W9-AIM-934

Nature's I.Q.

Balázs Hornyánszky — István Tasi

Nature's I.Q.

Copyright © 2009 (English Edition)
Originally published in Hungarian
© Balázs Hornyánszky, István Tasi, 2002

All right reserved. No part of this book may be reproduced, stored in a retieval system
or transmitted in any form, by any means, including mechanical, electronic, photocopying,
recording, or otherwise, without the prior written consent of the publisher.

First English Printing 2009
Printed in India

Contributors: Csaba Kuron, Dániel Keszthelyi, Edina Fodor, Ferenc Farkas,
Gábor Szűcs, Gábor Tóth, Mónika Jegyernik, László Répássy, Orsolya Németh

Design: Zsuzsa Magyar

Layout works:
Pozitív Logika Grafikai Stúdió

Library of Congress Cataloging-in-Publication Data

Tasi, Istvan, 1970–
  Nature's I.Q. : extraordinary animal behaviors that defy evolution / by
Istvan Tasi and Balazs Hornyanszky.
      p. cm.
  Includes bibliographical references.
  ISBN 978-0-9817273-0-1
  1. Animal behavior. 2. Evolution (Biology) I. Hornyanszky, Balazs. II.
Title.
  QL751.T29 2009
  591.5—dc22

                         2008035100

Attention Colleges, Universities, Associations and Professional Organizations: *Nature's IQ,*
is available at special discounts for bulk purchases for fund-raising or educational use.
Special books, booklets, or excerpts can be created to suit your specific needs.

Torchlight Publishing Inc.
PO Box 52
Badger CA 93603
www.torchlight.com
Email: torchlightpublishing@yahoo.com

Nature's I.Q.

Contents

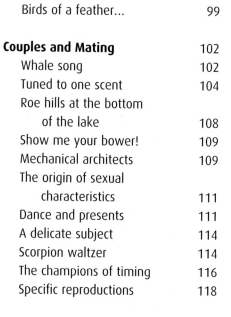

"Whence is it that Nature doth nothing in vain; and whence arises all that order and beauty which we see in the world?... How came the bodies of animals to be contrived with so much art, and for what ends were their several parts? Was the eye contrived without skill in optics, and the ear without knowledge of sounds? How do the motions of the body follow from the will, and whence is the instinct in animals?"

Isaac Newton

Foreword

Nature's IQ is a beautiful book. The pictures are beautiful, the words are beautiful, the ideas are beautiful. As one goes through the pages of *Nature's IQ*, one is confronted with one example after another of the delicate organic and behavioral complexity of living things.

This complexity of life is so stunning that before Darwin most scientists were prepared to believe that it could be explained only by appealing to an intelligent designer, God. The few who did not like the idea of such a designer could present no credible alternative. When he published *The Origin of Species*, Darwin gave such scientists hope that the wonderful complexity of living things could be explained without appealing to an intelligent designer. He proposed that biological complexity and diversity could possibly be explained by variations in populations of living things. Only the living things possessing the variations that made them fitter than others would survive in nature. Thus variation and natural selection, proposed Darwin, could explain the diversity and complexity of living things. One hundred and fifty years later, this promise has failed to come true. Scientists have come to understand that the principal source of variety in living things resides in their genes. Change in physical form and behavior is thus rooted in the genes of living things. Genetic change is the source of variation. But to this day, scientists are unable to specify the exact series of genetic changes necessary to produce the marvelously complex organic structures and behaviors illustrated in this beautiful book nor show how natural selection alone could account for them.

Nature's IQ confronts us with many wonders of nature that Darwinists have failed to explain in any strictly scientific fashion. They simply ask us to believe that somehow or other it all happened by evolution. The authors of *Nature's IQ* give us good reasons to no longer accept Darwinian fairy tales as actual explanations. They demonstrate to us that truly scientific explanations have not been given, and that in principle, they cannot be given.

The authors of *Nature's IQ* breathe new life into the design argument in biology, particularly in regard to the complex behaviors displayed by many living things. These complex behaviors involve many behavioral steps, linked in specific sequences. Without each step being present in proper sequence, the complete behavior would not be executed. We can thus say that not only biological form but also biological behavior can be irreducibly complex. That means these behaviors cannot have arisen in the step by step fashion that natural selection requires. Thus biological behavior also provides evidence of intelligent design. This book is bound to become a classic, taking its place alongside the works of Michael Behe and William Dembski in the modern intelligent design movement.

Michael A. Cremo
Author *Human Devolution: A Vedic Alternative to Darwin's Theory*
Coauthor *Forbidden Archeology: The Hidden History of the Human Race*

October 15, 2008
Los Angeles

7

ntroduction

Apparently it is not at all surprising that ants behave like ants, birds behave like birds, and mammals behave like mammals. They execute most of their eating, defending, and mating activities in a predetermined instinctive way. But how do the animals know when and how they should do what they do?

Where does nature's I.Q. come from? Our book, as its title indicates, seeks the answer to the following question: What is the cause of the "practical" bodily structure of living beings and the intelligent behavior going along with it? Since animals are more expressive than plants, we took most of our examples from the behavior of animals (although we are aware that the vegetable kingdom also abounds with interesting features).

The situation-assessing and problem-solving abilities of human beings differ from one individual to another. These abilities can be numerically expressed by the I.Q. (intelligence quotient), the unit measuring human intelligence. Different animal species and groups are also equipped with specific problem-solving abilities; however, most of these work not in a conscious, but in an automatic hereditary way. Where does this encoded intelligence come from? Can the currently widespread view really be true— that the mass of inert matter (lacking consciousness) somehow acquired intelligence over the course of an immensely long time? Does nature possess innate intelligence? Or does our world reflect in many different ways a supernatural, external intelligence that applied its own infinitely ingenious solutions in creating the living world?

As Darwin believed it

About 150 years ago, Charles Darwin quite stoutly questioned the creationist view. In his work *The Origin of Species* (1859), he treated the possibility of species evolving from one another in detail. The process he conceived and outlined became widely known as evolution. Darwin argued for the validity of his theory using data from the realms of domestication, geology, morphology, embryology, and the geographical division of species. However, all data he mentioned can also be explained according to traditional, religious worldviews. Darwin's success rested not so much in the overwhelming validity of his theory, but in the fact that the society of his age had already more or less revolted against the religious worldview and the supremacy of the Church and was seeking to create an all-encompassing materialistic worldview. So the emergence of Darwin's theory, which was devoid of anything transcendental, was timely, although it contained many shortcomings.

For the reader to follow the argumentation of this book, a brief examination of the basis of the Darwinian theory of evolution in connection with the origin of species is worthwhile. The basic tenet of the theory is that because the quantity, habitat, and available food of plants and animals are limited, there is competition for them. From time to time, within any given species, an organism emerges that slightly differs from other members of the same species. These

Innovative
Predators

Innovative Predators

14

Welcome to our exploration of the mysteries of animal behavior. First we will examine how animal instincts work in the course of food acquisition. An especially interesting question concerns the origin of intelligent animal behavior in this regard. If one examines the feeding habits of animals, one sometimes finds an extremely sophisticated use of tools (often part of the animal's own body). The complexity and uniqueness of both the tools and the special behavior pattern in which they are used strongly suggest that such feeding phenomena could not possibly have developed by evolution.

Deceptive hunters

In nature we find many animals who disguise themselves and use one of their limbs as a lure to attract their prey. A perfect example is the deep-sea anglerfish (*Linophryne arborifera*), which lives more than twenty-four hundred feet below the surface, in total darkness. Above its mouth is a strange, thin appendage with a wide end that emits a green glow. Unlike most fish, the angler doesn't swim after its prey. Instead, it waits, and by slowly moving the bioluminescent bulb on its head, it lures its prey within range. When an unsuspecting little fish swims close to the fascinating light, the anglerfish snatches it.

The question is: How could this luminescent lure and the behavior pattern coupled to it develop gradually? The theory of evolution states that the anglerfish must have evolved from a normal fish, i.e., from one that lacked any strange headdress and, like ordinary fish, got its daily meal by chasing smaller fish. But just how did this evolution occur?

The usual explanation is that new species evolve from established species slowly, step

by step, over many, many generations. It is supposed that in the animal world individuals are sometimes born with minor variations caused by random genetic mutations. If a new trait gives the organism some advantage over its peers, it will more likely survive and reproduce. And as these beneficial traits accumulate over a long, long time, an organism will develop new organs, features, and abilities. However, we will see that in many cases this proposed scenario makes no sense.

First of all, no one has ever observed any mutation that caused a new organ to appear or enhanced the functions of an existing one. In fact, mutations often prove fatal. At best, a mutation turns out to be neutral, i.e., it doesn't cause the organism any trouble during its life but also doesn't help it.

The theory of gradual development fails to explain many existing features in organisms because these features are advantageous only in their present, finished form; the intermediate stages in a hypothetical development chain would have been useless

in the genes, and acquired traits mostly develop due to the influence of the environment and learning. Scientific research also reveals that behavioral patterns previously thought to be solely instinctive and hereditary often contain elements that were acquired or learned during ontogeny. For example, members of certain fish species of the family of cichlids (*Cichlidae*) learn at the time of the first spawning that they only have to take care of offspring that belong to their own species. If we mislead a young couple by replacing their first spawns with the roes of a different species, the couple will accept and bring up the extraneous broods and will never take care of their own "blood" offspring born afterward; moreover, they will kill them. In other words, cichlids have the propensity and ability to take care of their offspring, but they learn what these spawns look like only at the time of the first spawning.

The discipline of ethology not only tries to describe the phenomena of the animal world but also tries to find an answer to the origin of the behavior of animals. Since the majority of researchers accept Darwin's theory of evolution and take it as their starting point, they try to account for the emergence of different forms of behavior with the help of a theory postulating that simpler behavioral forms underwent a gradual, step-by-step change. However, when we try to deduce the "evolution" of specific animal activities in this way, it turns out that it is impossible! In our book, following the description of specific phenomena, we examine the basic hypotheses of scientists, who are specialists of this field, about the origin of the behavior of certain animals. And we find that on reflection these assumptions do not hold water. Naturally it is not possible to deal with every evolutionary view; therefore, we only examine the most common views concerning the development of the given phenomenon.

Sometimes it may seem we are arguing against Charles Darwin alone. However, one should be aware that although the theory of evolution has undergone considerable changes in details—today there are many different, albeit contradictory, explanations of the speed, the main forces, and the whys and wherefores of the supposed process of evolution—these modern speculations have never denied the basic Darwinian assumption, namely that species have evolved from one another. Therefore, our most important arguments against Darwin are equally valid against the evolutionists of the present time and are relevant to the hypotheses propagated by them.

Finally, we would like to point out that whenever we may hear or read about the "evolutionary explanations" of different phenomena (even those mentioned in this book), we should treat them with reservations; these are not scientifically demonstrated statements but merely unproven ideas. We should clearly separate nature's tangible facts from speculative explanations or hypotheses. If we fail to do so, we can easily become prey to ideological manipulation in the guise of science. After thoroughly analyzing the examples presented in this book, the natural conclusion is that the postulation of a step-by-step evolution of species from one to the other does not stand. It is quite possible that an intelligent designer plays the leading role in the formation of the anatomy and behavior of animals. This possibility we leave to the reader to decide.

11

12

About the authors

The authors of the book are Balázs Hornyánszky, bio-engineer, and István Tasi, cultural anthropologist. Balázs Hornyánszky collected and analyzed most of the examples in the book. István Tasi assisted in composing the examples and arranging them into a book format, as well as in writing the last chapter. Mónika Jegyernik, a medical student, continuously assisted us in our work. All work as teachers and researchers in the Vedic Science Research Center, the aim of which is studying and teaching Indian Vaishnava culture. The Research Center compares the culture and philosophy of Vaishnavism with its Western counterparts and the results of different disciplines of our day in many fields. The object of scrutiny in *Nature's IQ* is the theory of evolution, the basis of contemporary biology and ethology. In the last chapter of the book, we briefly present the Vedic view on the origin of species and the behavior of animals.

The style of the book models popular works so it will be comprehensible not only to biologists but for the layperson as well. For our readers trained in sciences, we suggest they keep an eye on the relevant scientific literature. Although here and now we do not have the possibility to thoroughly analyze every phenomenon, we are certain that unbiased research in this field will sooner or later verify our basic assumption about natural design and the higher origin of the living world.

Acknowledgements

Before we delve into the analysis of nature's instincts, we would like to thank our spiritual master, H. H. Shivarama Swami, for directing our attention to the topic of this book through his exciting and instructive lectures. We are very grateful to Dr. Ottó Merkl, Ph.D., Director of the fauna collection of the Hungarian Museum of Natural Science. Although his views on the origin of the living world differ from ours, he gave us invaluable help in identifying the species described in the book and in correcting the inaccuracies of certain zoological examples. We owe many thanks to several Hungarian nature photographers and leaders of the Art Association of Hungarian Nature Photographers for granting us the use of their pictures. With the help of all mentioned above, we hope we have created a book that is delightful, entertaining, and thought provoking.

The deep-sea anglerfish lures its prey with its light organ. Could the lamp and the behavior matching it have emerged by a series of accidents?

or often harmful. To illustrate, let's return to our deep-sea anglerfish. Let's imagine a fish that did not have a luminescent bulb in the middle of its forehead. Instead, the first spoke of its dorsal fin—from which, says the theory of evolution, the appendage must have somehow developed—was completely normal. Let's suppose that a random genetic mutation caused minor changes in the first spoke of the dorsal fin: it became a little longer or a little wider, or maybe it got placed a little more forward. This slight change in the dorsal fin would not benefit the fish in the least, since it would not attract any smaller fish. And since this feature would not give the fish an advantage in survival over other fish of the same species, the process of natural selection would not come into play to create the new species of anglerfish. And even if somehow the fish with the slightly changed

dorsal fin mutated again so that the fin grew slightly longer, this longer appendage would still be useless and thus not enhance survival.

We should also note that the anglerfish's lamp is not just a simple protuberance. It contains rare bacteria that produce luminescent chemicals. This fact further reduces the chance that this "chemical factory" developed on its own through a series of chance events that one day all of sudden produced a little radiant club.

If by some miracle the appendage grew longer and longer throughout the generations and at one point started emitting light above the eyes of our deep-sea anglerfish, this organ would still fail to confer the least advantage on the fish. Why? Because any advantage presupposes a suitable behavior pattern—the anglerfish's slow waving of the bulb and its patient waiting for an

16

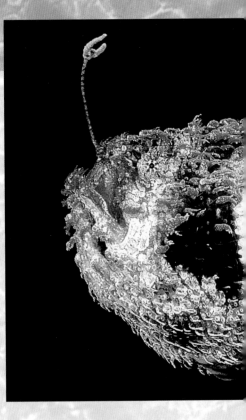

unsuspecting little fish to be attracted by the light. How would a fish endowed with an average fish's rudimentary intelligence know what behavior would best match his newly luminescent crest? If our prospective anglerfish chased after the smaller fish (behavior we would expect from a hungry predator), it would be immediately exposed and the "lighthouse" would become a definite *dis*advantage, acting as a warning to the prey.

From all this we must conclude that the luminescent appendage atop the fish's head had to appear all at once, in its complete form, together with the appropriate behavior. Such a radical change in form and behavior is impossible by way of evolution. Common sense rather demands that our anglerfish appeared as it exists now, equipped with all its special apparatus and knowledge, because of the planning of a higher intelligence.

We find many similar examples in the living world, even among other anglerfish. The Sargassum anglerfish (*Histrio histrio*), for example, attracts its victims by waving a fake morsel of food (actually the first spoke of its dorsal fin) while disguised to look as if covered by seaweed. If the logic of evolution were correct, the Sargassum anglerfish would need to have developed not only the modified fin but also the behavioral change enhancing its disguise. We cannot help but smile as we imagine a fish that catches its prey by quickly chasing it but whose offspring are equipped with a fin imitating a piece of flesh and a body that looks as if it's covered with seaweed—and all due to chance mutations, either suddenly or through a series of changes. Of course, this

is not the end of the story. This mutant fish would also need to have simultaneously learned how to behave so as to make its newly acquired form effective. When hungry, instead of dashing off in pursuit of prey as its forebears did, it would have to remain in one place while slowly moving its fin in imitation of a piece of flesh, and wait until the prey swims close to it!

The decoy scorpion fish (*Iracundus signifer*) uses an even more refined trick. Its dorsal fin looks and moves like a little fish that is its natural food, and the decoy is so realistic that the fishes it resembles mistake it for a female of their own species. When the decoy attracts a male who wishes to mate, the hopeful courter ends up in the scorpion fish's maw instead. Amazingly, when the scorpion fish is full it changes the color of the decoy so that the lusty little male fishes are no longer attracted. A theory positing the

Humans are not the only ones who use fishing rods. Anglerfish too have their own special fishing rod. But who invented it?

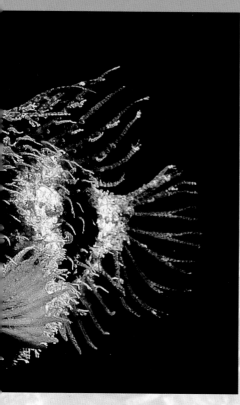

the bottom of ponds or streams and waits for a small fish to see the "worm" and swim into its mouth. This behavior could not have developed through a slow learning process. How would a turtle know that its tongue reminds small edible fish of a worm? And why would it open its mouth wide and sit in one place? Even if a highly gifted (or very lazy) turtle had done so in the past, this behavior would not have appeared in its offspring, because acquired behavioral patterns are not inherited. Abilities an organism acquires through learning or practice do not affect the organism's genetic material and thus are not passed on to its offspring, just as the knowledge we acquire during our studies is not passed on to our children. So the alligator snapping turtle's special daytime feeding behavior—to open its mouth wide and become motionless—must be a reflex, not a result of conditioning. The

17

On seeing such complex behavior in animals, one must conclude that a superior intelligence created them.

step-by-step evolution of the decoy scorpion fish faces the same problems we saw with previous examples. Moreover, in this case the decoy's change of color, which occurs in a particular neural and chemical way, makes the situation even more complex. This structural and chemical complexity reduces the chance of evolution by mutation to near zero.

We find similar cases in freshwater fishes as well. Certain species of silure, for instance, use their wormlike barb as a lure. We could say that they simply take advantage of the lucky similarity between their barb and certain worms. But how are the silure fish aware of this similarity right from birth?

Among land reptiles and amphibians we find even more intricate feeding habits. The small bulge on the tongue of the alligator snapping turtle (Macroclemys temminckii) resembles a worm. During the day this snapper rests with its mouth wide open on

18

behavior is obviously coded into the animal's genes and is therefore inherited. The most reasonable explanation for the emergence of the alligator snapping turtle is therefore not that it evolved from another species but that it appeared in the distant past with the same form and habits it has today.

The Argentine horned frog (*Ceratophrys cornuta*) uses one of the toes on a hind foot

The Argentine horned frog lures insects by moving its longest hind toe. Did he invent this technique—or was he invented?

as a lure. The frog moves its toe slowly and waits for it to attract an insect. The copperhead snake (*Agkistrodon contortrix*) uses its wormlike tail as a lure. The slowly squirming tip of its tail is irresistible to the curious and unsuspecting frogs that happen to pass by. When a frog fails to notice that the squirming worm is connected to a snake, the copperhead snatches it at the right moment. In these cases, animals use various organs as lures to acquire food. But it is only in their present state that these organs can perform that function. Any hypothetical intermediary

stage would have been useless and therefore could not have helped the new species develop through the famous Darwinian processes of survival of the fittest and natural selection. To help our odd species survive, these organs had to appear in their complete form—not gradually, over a long period. Moreover, as pointed out above, even possessing the complete organ for luring prey will not help unless accompanied by a completely new behavior pattern quite distinct from the usual alimentary habits of related species. We propose, therefore, that it is a higher intelligence that equipped these animals with the appropriate lures and "programmed" them with matching behavior.

If you're hungry, I'll eat you!

Our second group of animals with amazing feeding habits consists of those who disguise *themselves* as their prey's food or mate and thus lure it within range.

Our first example is the Malaysian orchid mantis (*Hymenopus coronatus*). The form and color of this mantis so strikingly resemble an orchid's that the human eye can hardly distinguish it from the real thing, even up close. The insect that happens to approach in search of pollen is in for a very

Like most spiders, the European garden spider waits patiently in its web for an insect to fall into its trap

But other species employ methods of survival that seem ready-made and could not have developed from one another

The copperhead uses a trick that may very well be the invention of a superior intelligence.

19

unpleasant surprise when it finds out that the beautiful flower is actually a greedy mantis.

The South American leaf fish (*Monocirrhus polyacanthus*) is the aquatic counterpart of the orchid-imitating mantis. This small fish lies motionless on a river bottom, looking like a harmless leaf. But the curious creature that ventures close is snatched with lightning speed and devoured.

The New Guinean dung spider (*Phrynarachne decipiens*) has developed this type of deceptive feeding practice even further. First of all, casting aside all vanity, it displays colors that perfectly mimic the droppings of a certain kind of bird, and therefore the spider doesn't have to fear attack from that bird. Moreover, the dung spider secretes a chemical that makes it also smell like bird droppings. This smell attracts certain flies and butterflies that feed on dung, and these become its food. In this case the question arises as to how and when the spider's

outer coating came to resemble bird droppings so closely, and how it developed the smell to match. This latter would entail genetic coding to be able to synthesize and transport the hormone responsible for the smell. In this case, as in the previous ones, one cannot conclude that a step-by-step evolution took place, since the intermediate steps would not have given the animal any evolutionary advantage. The spider needs to display a very complex color pattern to trick the birds into thinking it is their own droppings. If in the beginning the spider had only slightly resembled the droppings, the birds would have seen through the attempted disguise and nipped the "evolutionary change" in the bud. Also, to lure the flies and butterflies, the substance that causes this spider's deceptive smell must be chemically nearly identical to the odor-causing substance of the bird droppings. Until that near-identity is reached, any smell the spider produced would give it absolutely no advantage. So where is the scope for gradual evolution?

Regarding all our above examples, one might suggest that the beneficial traits appeared suddenly as a result of a massive genetic mutation. First, the probability of such a mutation is nearly zero, and second, the great genetic difference between the

20

new specimen and the old members of its species would be so great that it would not be able to mate with them, reproduce, and pass on the new traits. Small, gradual changes, on the other hand, would not confer any benefit; therefore, such individuals would not survive and would soon disappear from the group.

However, there is a very simple explanation for how the Malaysian orchid mantis, South American leaf fish, and New Guinean dung spider acquired such extraordinary features. According to this theory, these wonderful animals did not develop by evolution. Their ancestors appeared long, long ago in the same form we see today, the creations of an intelligent being.

Animal cutlery

Our third group of animals with extraordinary feeding behavior consists of those whose ability to acquire food depends on their use of tools or other items they find in their environment. Many people are surprised to learn of these creatures because the common belief is that only humans can use tools. So, the question is: Did these animals discover how to use the tools, applying their own intelligence to solve a critical problem of food acquisition, or is their behavior based on instinct, which impels them to act in a certain way that happens to include the use of tools?

Our first example is the Egyptian vulture (*Neophron percnopterus*), which repeatedly throws stones on an ostrich egg until the shell breaks and the contents become accessible. As usual, our question is: Where

does this exceptional food-acquiring method come from? How did it arise? According to adherents of the evolution theory, long, long ago the Egyptian vulture's ancestors lacked this special ability. But over the eons, through many generations, the present species developed it.

Let us consider this explanation. The Egyptian vulture cannot break the ostrich eggs with its beak. The ability to recognize the eggs and the impulse to search for stones are inherited traits. We know this because an experiment was performed in which a baby vulture was taken from its parents and raised alone. This vulture became agitated when it saw a large egg and immediately looked for stones (it even flew away to find some), and when it had them it threw them on the egg. Obviously, the isolated vulture could not have learned this behavior from its parents or peers. At its first encounter with an egg it began haphazardly throwing stones at it. After one of the stones hit the egg and broke it, the bird would always aim in the direction of the egg, until finally nearly all the stones it threw hit the target. Learning played a part only in refining the behavior; the basic activities were controlled by instinct. The isolation experiment shows that the vulture's egg-breaking mechanism—looking for stones upon seeing an egg and then throwing them at the egg—is an inherited ability.

But how and when did this inherited ability appear in this species? The evolutionists say there are two possibilities. One is that at some time in the past a vulture somehow discovered it. As we have already pointed out, however, a learned ability cannot be inherited because it has no effect

The bearded vulture breaks the bones of dead animals by dropping them on a stony surface to get to their marrow.

Where does the "program" of the Egyptian vulture's complex egg-breaking technique come from?

on the individual's genes. Since today we see that this behavior is certainly inherited from one generation of Egyptian vultures to the next, it must be encoded in the genes and brain of each individual. So this possibility can be ruled out. The second possibility, say the evolutionists, is that this ability developed through chance mutations. According to the logic of natural selection, based on survival of the fittest, this second possible explanation can be valid only if each intermediate change is more beneficial than the previous ones. But the phenomena that constitute the special feeding behavior of the

Certain animals use one of their limbs as a tool to acquire food. The great egret, for instance, harpoons prey with its beak. Other animals even use actual tools—thorns, for instance—but most probably not because of their own ingenuity.

Egyptian vulture—the search for stones upon seeing the ostrich egg, the retrieval of the stones, and the repeated casting of the stones upon the egg—would be meaningless and useless if all of them were not present and fully developed at the same time. It is worth noting that the Egyptian vulture lives among several other vulture species, but these vultures never acquire the ability to throw stones and break open ostrich eggs. They do not even attempt it, no matter how often they see it performed.

Therefore we can conclude that the complicated series of activities constituting the stone-throwing behavior of the Egyptian vulture is a system of irreducible complexity that could not have evolved gradually. The theory of evolution simply cannot explain how this instinctive behavior could have developed over time.

We see another interesting feeding technique in the bearded vulture (*Gypaetus barbatus*), which breaks bones to get to the delicious marrow within. To accomplish this, it will take a bone in its beak, carry it high into the air, and then drop it onto a stony surface. Remarkably, after ingesting the marrow, this vulture also eats the bone fragments as well, its gastric juices being so strong that it can easily digest them.

We find a hereditary use of tools in the small cactus finch (*Geospiza scandens*),

which feeds on insects that burrow into tree trunks. Because its beak is unsuitable for poking the insects from the trunks, the cactus finch uses a sharp object, most often a cactus thorn.

The hereditary feeding behavior of one species of assassin bug is even more spectacular. This insect places dead ants, remains of other insects, and grains of sand on itself as a disguise. Ants regularly remove their dead fellows from the anthill, and so they walk into the trap and become the assassin bug's victims. In this case it is out of the question that the process could have been learned. How would an insect know that if it places all kinds of litter along with dead ants upon itself and walks to the middle of an anthill and remains there patiently, the ants will naturally be attracted to it so it can easily eat them? The idea of gradual development by way of mutations cannot hold in this case either, because of the same arguments mentioned in the case of the stone-throwing vulture: the behavior is useful only in its complete form; its separate elements are useless in themselves.

Earlier we raised the question of whether the abovementioned animals' intriguing techniques for procuring food are proof of extraordinary intelligence, in either the individual or the species. Can we say that the egg-breaking or bone-breaking vulture or the bug that covers itself with dead ants is especially clever? The answer is obviously no. These animals do not acquire their skills by themselves. The skills are innate, part of their genetic program, or instincts. Therefore, we should give all credit to some other intelligence besides theirs.

It would be difficult to attribute the extraordinary behavior of the archerfish to blind chance, for it fires a "water cannon" even in mid-air if necessary. How would a fish that lived long ago suddenly think of spitting above the water's surface? If it had not already possessed a mouth structure appropriate for this, what would have been the benefit?

Knowledge ready-made

Let's now consider a few more examples of animals with exceptional feeding habits. Before eating a captured wasp, the honey buzzard (*Pernis apivorus*) and some other bird species tear out its stinger. Honey buzzards raised apart from their parents and fellow birds also behave like this, which means that the behavior is hereditary. They would not have time to learn it anyway, because if a wasp stings their throat only once, they die. Therefore, theories referring to the step-by-step evolution of this behavior are false.

The bird known as the greater honeyguide (*Indicator indicator*) cannot get honey from a beehive by itself, so it will guide a bigger animal such as a honey badger to the beehive with its persistent chirping. After the badger extracts the honeycomb and eats its fill, it yields the honeycomb, the larvae, and the remaining honey to the greater honeyguide. Like all the other exceptional feeding habits we've mentioned, this type of behavior by the honeyguide is hereditary. Its emergence raises the same problems as before. How would a honeyguide nestling know how to get honey? It has to have this knowledge in totality right from birth, so no step-by-step evolution makes any sense.

Finally, let us examine the case of the archerfish (*Toxotes jaculator*). From under water this fish shoots insects at rest with a stream of water. Or sometimes the archerfish will jump out of the water and spit on a selected victim, which then falls into the water and becomes easy prey for the archerfish.

The archerfish is the champion of target-spitting. Could it have possibly been missing its target for millennia before it evolved its present-day deadeye marksmanship?

24

The body of the archerfish is flat on the sides, and its huge eyes and mouth point upward. The water jet ready to be shot is compressed in the pharynx, which is pressed against a slot on the fish's palate, on the fleshy part of its tongue. Young specimens even have colorful spots to attract the insects. It is also worth noting that the fish very seldom misses its target, even if it shoots from under water, often from a yard below the surface. It should miss the target more frequently because of light refraction. But because it is very accurate, we can conclude that the fish takes refraction into account. We should note that this aquatic animal's anatomy is very special. As if with a squirt gun, it very expertly shoots the unsuspecting insects with its mouth apparatus, which is perfectly adapted for this purpose. Its special mouth is coupled with a very unusual behavior. The parallel, long-term gradual evolution of all these capabilities is absolutely unlikely. A fish spitting haphazardly in all directions with a half-developed mouth would have no advantage over ordinary specimens. We therefore have to conclude that the archerfish is also a very successful construction that has always existed in its present form.

From these examples it is clear that there are many examples of food-acquisition phenomena whose emergence cannot be satisfactorily explained by any of the present varieties of the theory of evolution. Like all animals, those described above have organs, abilities, and behavior patterns that enable them to acquire suitable food. In our view, these complex food-acquiring methods could not have developed through a step-by-step evolution from simpler forms. It seems much more likely that all species are equipped by a higher intelligence with organs, instincts, and abilities that enable them to acquire food from their surroundings and thus maintain their physical existence. We may note that this intelligent designer appears to have an endless number of novel ideas and a very good sense of humor. His creatures can adapt to their environments to a certain extent, but they did not evolve from other species and will never develop into new species.

Defense, disguise, deception

Defense, Disguise, Deception

Now let's examine the feeding process from the opposite perspective, that of the potential prey. Certain animals improve their chance of escaping their enemies because of their color or the special marks on their bodies, while others elude predators by employing artful tricks and defensive maneuvers. Our analysis will seek to determine the origin of these defensive measures. Could the process of evolution have created these measures by means of nature's blind laws of mutation and natural selection? Did the ancestors of today's species invent them? Or should we search elsewhere for their origin?

26

Expressive colors and marks

Colors or marks on an animal's body can relay a warning to a predator or convey some other information. For instance, some animals warn their enemies that they are poisonous in this way. Central and South America are the homes of at least twenty frog species whose skin secretes a poison that is lethal if it enters the bloodstream. The poison will immediately paralyze a bird or even a monkey. Natives often collect the poison and smear it on the tips of the darts they use for tribal warfare or hunting. Hence the name "poison-dart frogs." The golden poison-dart frog (*Phyllobates terribilis*) is one of the most venomous. Less than an ounce of this frog's poison could kill the population of a medium-sized city, making it one of the most fearsome poisons in nature. All poison frogs display vivid colors—yellow-black, golden, scarlet, bright green, crimson. Equipped with their bright warning colors, these frogs,

Poison-dart frogs warn predators of their toxicity with their striking colors.

unlike most, are active during the day rather than at night. In their vivid shirts they confidently jump everywhere, in forest trees and other foliage and on the ground. If a predator still wants to taste one of them, the extremely unpleasant experience will certainly discourage him from a second try. When the poison reaches the stomach it may not be lethal, but it will certainly cause a memorable bout of indigestion. So

predators have learned to leave alone the bright-colored members of the "untouchable" frog caste. Perhaps it was nature's intelligent arranger who took care to protect these species by equipping them with a strong poison and characteristic color combinations to warn of this.

More interesting than poison frogs are poison species that ward off predators without the predators ever having tasted them, i.e., without any prior experience. Consider the poisonous sea snake, for example. The vividly marked sea snake is one of the most poisonous snakes living in the Indian and Pacific oceans. Experiments have shown that predator fish living in the same area do not touch these snakes, even if they have never encountered them before. Avoidance of the deadly prey is an inherited feature.

Let's stop here for a moment. How do these inexperienced predator fish know that sea snakes with distinctive marks are poisonous? Despite lacking any experience of them (so there can be no question of learning), a predator fish will still refrain from attacking such snakes when it comes upon them for the first time. Learning is out

of the question simply because one bite would finish off the predator fish, and it would have no opportunity to make good use of its experience. Is it conceivable that the ancestors of these predator fish suddenly had random mutant offspring whose genes whispered to them, "Never eat brightly colored, vividly marked sea snakes"? This is obviously absurd. So no matter how mystical it seems, the predator fish must be driven by instincts that were encoded into the genes of that species at the very beginning of its existence. How? By means of a plan put into effect by a higher intelligence. This plan makes it possible for members of a given species to know from birth which organisms it should treat as food and which it should avoid.

"Keep your eyes open"

Some organisms sport pseudo eyes that mislead their attackers. These eyespots are often quite lifelike, with shading and glittering highlights that give them an almost hypnotizing effect. Certain fish,

Predator fish do not attack or harm the poisonous sea snakes even when encountering them for the first time. But if the fish never tasted them, how do they know these snakes are dangerous?

28

insects, caterpillars, snakes, and birds resort to this trick. A fake pair of eyes can create the illusion that an animal is bigger than it really is, thus frightening away predators. Some fish who inhabit coral reefs display an eyespot on their tail or dorsal fin so that if their enemies do strike they will attack less vulnerable parts than the head. The copper-band butterfly fish (*Chelmon rostratus*) even swims backwards to enhance the ruse.

Many butterflies and moths sport dramatic eyespots on their wings. One example is the eyed hawk-moth (*Smerinthus ocellata*). When this moth is at rest, its front pair of wings covers its rear pair, concealing

The eyespots on these butterflies' wings become very useful in case of attack.

The copper-band butterfly fish has eyes even on its back that divert the attention of predators from its head. This fish can even swim in reverse, which makes the phenomenon even more credible!

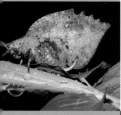

This katydid species resembles a leaf. Did it adapt itself, or has someone else adapted it to its environment?

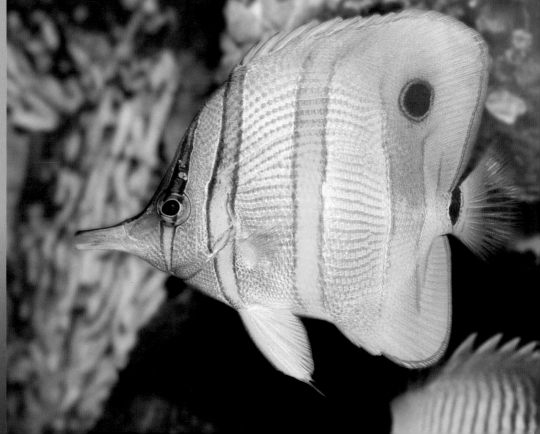

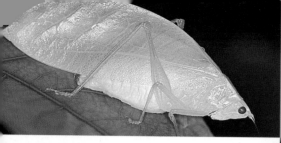

Some species look like certain elements of their environment—a leaf or a twig, for example. One could very easily argue that the same designer who shaped the leaf and the twig created such species, too. The female katydid resembles a leaf. It flashes its hind wing covered with vivid colors and patterns in case of danger. Its exterior and interior patterns are perfectly in tune with its "duplicitous" behavior.

the eyespots and making the moth less visible. But when attacked, it quickly flashes the frightening imitation eyes to scare off the attacker. A similar ploy is used by the leaf-mimicking katydid (*Typophyllum bolivari*), which inhabits the Peruvian jungles. In a state of rest it resembles a parched leaf, but when confronted with danger it flashes its rear pair of wings, which display vivid marks and dazzling white spots. The attacking bird or lizard usually departs quickly in fear.

Adherents of the theory of evolution would say that insects with eyespots and other vivid wing patterns developed via natural selection from those having wings without eyespots and of homogeneous color. This explanation presupposes that insects' wings are constantly being transformed, through mutation, into wings with different colors and marks so that natural selection can act and the fittest insects can survive and reproduce. But our observations do not confirm this scenario. Insects with wings of a certain pattern produce offspring with virtually identical wing patterns. The slight variations are so insignificant that they provide no advantage of survival whatsoever; consequently they cannot be a source of further transformations. In other words, we have no proof at all that the ancestors of insects with eyespots did not have eyespots.

A further problem with the theory of gradual evolution is that the wing ornaments are often coupled with inherited behavior that enhances their effectiveness. In other words, from birth the insect knows what effect its marks will produce in predators and deploys its camouflage at the opportune moment and in the best way to

scare them off. According to evolutionists, not only did the wing ornaments develop by a series of random genetic mutations, but so did the behavioral patterns appropriate for the ornaments. The probability of such parallel series of random mutations producing the many insect species with effective eyespots is practically nil. It's much more reasonable to conclude that an intelligent guiding force originally equipped the insects with the eyespots and the behavior that makes them effective defensive mechanisms.

Bluff for survival

One way an animal can escape from predators is to appear to be something entirely different. For example, some organisms deceive hungry predators by seeming to be much bigger than an ideal bite. Others disguise themselves as excrement or as an organism the predator regards as dangerous.

One example of such extreme disguise is the South American four-eyed frog (*Pleurodema bibroni*). On its rump this frog has two imitation eyes that seem to stare at the observer. These are not just eyespots; they're large nodes—perfect imitations of real eyes, complete with spots for pupils. This frog will confidently defend itself against an attacking hungry snake by

About face! The "eyes" on the backside of these frogs provide them some protection by scaring off predators.

The grass snake pretends to be dead when confronted with danger. The fixed and predetermined nature of its behavioral program is proven by the fact that if we turn it to normal position in this state, it immediately turns back and assumes the death-feigning posture again.

abruptly turning its back while pressing its head to the ground and lifting its rump so that its two fake eyes stare at the aggressor. Simultaneously, the frog changes color by activating the brown, black, blue, gray, and white spots on its skin. Moreover, the frog's flexed hind legs resemble a huge mouth, and the tip of its body mimics a pointed nose—everything is in exactly the right position! When the frog presses its front legs close to its body, the two hind legs are lifted a little bit off the ground. Then these flexed, protruding legs resemble deadly claws. The whole show is more than enough to convince the snake to beat a quick retreat and look for a less risky dinner candidate.

Our inevitable question: Where did the fake eyes on the frog's rump come from? Traditional evolutionary theory says they must have developed gradually, obeying the crack of the whip of natural selection. In that case, however, the first appearance of what would develop into the eye-nodes would have been tiny protuberances a predator would hardly notice. Such small blemishes would result in no survival advantage at all. According to the evolutionists' view, any new feature that doesn't provide any survival advantage to the organism disappears over the generations; it does not develop further through thousands of small steps into something that, at last, would be useful. Then could the fake eyes have appeared suddenly as a result of a single mutation, in exactly the right position and with the right markings? No, this is next to impossible, especially if we consider that the frog "knows" what mask it has and behaves accordingly, i.e., it doesn't try to escape its attacker but turns its back on him

and lifts its rump-mask menacingly. This means its behavior is also hereditary. The simultaneous appearance, via chance mutation, of the pseudo eyes, the ability to change color, and the knowledge of just what to do at precisely the right moment is, to put it mildly, highly improbable. It is as if someone born with a Mona-Lisa–shaped mole on his or her back were also to know from birth Leonardo DaVinci's biography.

Again, the modern version of the evolution theory cannot explain the origin of such species as the South American four-eyed frog. Maybe it would be worthwhile to

consider a new explanation based on different axioms.

Now let's examine another example of extreme disguise. More than one hungry bird has been scared off when a caterpillar that appeared to be a tasty morsel suddenly lifted its rear end from the leaf it was resting on and displayed what looked like a frightening snake-head, complete with protruding tongue. The caterpillar of the Great Mormon butterfly (*Papilio memnon*), a native of the Asian and North Australian tropics, defends

It is unable to understand that it reveals itself by its movement. Therefore, it is probable that the death-feigning trick is not its own invention, but was programmed into it by a higher intelligence.

itself like this. It has eyelike growths on its tail that make the tail look exactly like a snake's head. The effect is further enhanced by its bifurcated, bright-red "tongue," which protrudes below the fake eyes. When threatened, the caterpillar lifts its rear end and begins to flap the "tongue," giving an excellent impression of an angry snake ready to attack, and for good measure it emits an extremely offensive smell. These

tactics provide a nearly foolproof defense against birds and small predators.

In this case also it seems extremely unlikely the defensive features could have developed through gradual, minute changes. If the tail had evolved through thousands of years in this way, it would have looked like a snake only in its fully developed form. Through all those thousands of years the tail would have provided no advantage what-

32

This frog looks exactly like the excrement of a bird. The tiny changes of its imagined "evolution" would not have given it any benefit of survival at the beginning stages.

soever to the caterpillar, and consequently, it could not have survived. The cases of the South American four-eyed frog and the snake-tailed caterpillar raise the possibility that these species exist as we know them today because of an artful plan. A caring, higher being could have easily equipped these animals with such features—along with suitable accompanying behavior—to improve their chances of survival.

Lurkers

Some organisms use extreme disguise to "hide in plain sight." For example, a species of leaf frog in Ecuador perfectly disguises itself as bird droppings. It even imitates the many-colored stripes of bird excrement. This frog has nothing to do but bask motionless on a sun-drenched leaf with its legs pressed tightly to its body. Unlike other frogs, it doesn't have to fear predators, since no self-respecting predator would deign to eating bird stool!

In one species of treehopper (*Umbonia spinosa*), the female's hump looks like the thorn of a rose, and if the insect flattens itself tightly against a branch, it seems part of the tree. On observing this insect, a proponent of evolution would triumphantly exclaim, "Ah, it has adapted itself to its environment!" But we would reply, "How could one possibly deduce or describe the process of such an adaptation?" If we start

with any other treehopper species and then postulate a series of small changes culminating in the insect's hump resembling a rose's thorn, it would take many generations for the resemblance to be close enough to protect the treehopper from its enemies. So there would be no group of treehoppers from which natural selection could select the ones developing the thorn-hump. It is thus very probable that this species of treehopper, like all treehoppers, was preplanned and did not develop over time. This assumption is supported by the fact that the male of this same species has a different kind of hump and its larvae have no hump at all.

The case of the Atlantic halibut (*Hippoglossus hippoglossus*) is also interesting. The most striking feature of this fish is its shape—not vertically oblong, like most fish, but horizontally flat, like a pancake. Actually,

A treehopper species is safe because its size and shape exactly resemble that of a rose thorn.

is caterpillar is only bluffing: its tail looks actly like a small snake sticking out its ngue. It even has false eyes. Logically it is conceivable that this complex form and havior would have developed through a ries of tiny, useful changes.

34

its shape is similar to that of other fish. It only looks flat because it spends most of its time lying on one side, hiding on the sandy sea floor. The fish is also special because its skin can take on the color of its environment; therefore, when lying on the sandy ocean bottom, it almost completely fades into the background. Scientists tested this imitative ability and found that when placed on a chessboard, a halibut was able to take on that pattern, too! One more oddity: both the halibut's eyes are on one side of its head, the upper side as it rests on the sea bottom. But how can a fish have both eyes on the same side of its body? At birth, the halibut's eyes are in the normal place, but as the fish grows, one eye gradually moves from one side to the other. In this way the grown-up fish has both eyes on its upper side as it peers from the sandy bottom—all the better to notice prey or predators.

It is very hard to imagine how the Ecuadorian leaf frog, the thorn-humped treehopper, and the Atlantic halibut described above developed from other species. These organisms' highly specialized disguises and matching behaviors are useful only in their present, complex form. Many generations of frogs only beginning to look like bird droppings would not enjoy the advantages of the disguise; consequently, there would not be any natural mechanism pushing further development along these lines. Similarly mysterious is the uniqueness of the shape of the treehoppers' thorn-hump and the anatomy of the Atlantic halibut, especially the eye that travels to the opposite side of the head as the fish grows up! This is undoubtedly a well-regulated and

Both eyes of halibuts are on the same side of their body. It is very difficult to think of such an anatomical oddity as being the product of gradual changes.

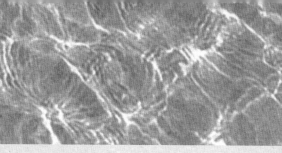

The stonefish looks like, and behaves, most of the time, like a stone, except when prey swims into its proximity.

complex physiological change with no conceivable intermediary versions.

Even Darwin himself struggled with this problem in *The Origin of Species*. How did both eyes of the Atlantic halibut get to the same side? Darwin tried to explain the phenomenon in the following way: The young Atlantic halibut, with eyes in the normal place, cannot stay in a vertical position for long. The fish soon becomes tired, lies on its side, and sinks to the bottom. Darwin observed that under such circumstances the fish tries to look upward even with the bottom eye, and thus the eye presses against the upper part of the eye socket. Observing this ocular habit of the halibut, Darwin further concluded that the still-flexible and cartilaginous skull of the growing halibut probably yielded to the pressure of the muscles, and in this way the shape of the head and the position of the eyes might

have undergone an irrevocable change. Following this pattern, the tendency of deformation might have increased generation after generation.

In light of modern biology, this explanation seems rather fantastic. Even if the strained goggling of a halibut lying its side had modified the position of its eyes, this mechanical modification, being an acquired feature, would not have been transmitted to its offspring. On the other hand, the strained goggling could modify the position of the eyes only by a few millimeters at most, although this too is just mere speculation. And the fact that one of its eyes could have initially stared at the bottom only a few millimeters farther away than normal would have provided no advantage at all in the survival of these fish. Therefore, this attempt at explaining the phenomenon is far from satisfactory, even according to evolution's own logic.

Moreover, once again, in our present examples the perfect camouflage is coupled with a specific behavior. This raises further problems. Even if we suppose that the above species evolved their disguises due to mutation, the creatures would not have known they were safe from predators. How would a mutant frog resembling bird droppings *know* that it resembles bird droppings and behave in such a way as to maximize the advantage of such a disguise? How would an accidentally evolved tree-hopper *know* that its hump resembled a thorn and then act in such a way as to become virtually indistinguishable from the branch it is resting on? And how could an Atlantic halibut *know* that its brilliant skin hides it from its enemies' view? How would

36

The Oriental fire-bellied toad (*Bombina orientalis*) is green from above, but if tossed, it automatically throws itself on its back and exhibits its red-patterned belly. This is how it warns its attacker that it is poisonous. It is as if someone had trained it: "In case of danger, flip over!"

these organisms know they do not have to flee in terror from predators because they are virtually invisible to them?

It seems most probable that these three hiding species appeared a long time ago in their present form, together with their present behavioral patterns, because of the actions of a higher intelligence.

The last throw

Now we will examine a few examples in which an animal's enemy has already noticed it and so deception is no longer possible. But the cause is not completely lost, because with good tactics and a "last throw," the worst can still be avoided. We have already seen in the case of the poison-dart frog how certain colors can warn off predators. Bright red, for instance, means danger. Poisonous animals often display a striking red, yellow, or black complexion, signaling to potential predators: "Watch out, I'm poisonous, don't eat me!" The fire-bellied toad (*Bombina bombina*) uses this tactic. When threatened, this toad quickly

falls flat on its back before the attacker and displays the red-and-black pattern on the lower part of its body. The attacker suddenly realizes the toad is poisonous and desists.

The toad's behavior is instinctive, i.e., it is coded in its genes. In other words, the animal doesn't have to think about what to do. Such instinctive behavior is a puzzle for adherents of evolution. How can the mindless process of natural selection account for such complex instinctive behavior? One attempted explanation is that some time in the distant past a toad invented a means to escape from its enemy by throwing itself on its back. But even if this happened, the toad could not have transmitted the defense reaction to its offspring, since acquired characteristics do not leave a trace in the genes, which determine hereditary characteristics. Consequently, the toad's offspring would not have known this trick. Still, generation after generation, each fire-bellied toad knows from birth how to ward off predators by falling on its back.

It is also difficult to conceive how the fire-bellied toad could have developed its

distinctive behavioral trait gradually, over several generations. The toad's falling on its back is effective only in its present form. The toad either assumes this pose and is saved, or it does not and dies. There are no intermediary stages.

pincushion. In this way it becomes not just frightening but also inedible.

Although the water-swallowing and inflating abilities of these two fish are not very complex, they are thought provoking. The anatomical structures that enable these

The fire-bellied toad sometimes turns up only its feet as a warning.

37

The puffer fish's ability to puff itself up requires the existence of many special physical features and abilities. Since these are beneficial only together, this species could not have developed step by step.

The northern puffer fish (*Spheroides maculatus*) and the spot-fin porcupine fish (*Diodon hystrix*) also use a peculiar defense mechanism: they suddenly increase their size significantly. When threatened, these fish swallow water, which they then press into a glove-like protrusion in the middle of their gut and retain. In addition, the spot-fin porcupine fish has dense spines on its skin. To repel predators it not only swells up but also transforms itself into a virtual

abilities differ markedly from those of the original fish from which the evolutionist would try to trace these species. The intestines with the glove-like protrusion are markedly different, what to speak of the skin of the porcupine fish.

One who attempts to explain these striking bodily traits and abilities by means of a step-by-step evolutionary process again gets caught in the net of logic. The imaginary puffer fish generations able to

38

There are snake species that are able to spit out their poison even long distances in the direction of the source of danger.

The short-horned lizard squirts blood from its eye onto the aggressor.

puff themselves up more and more wouldn't enjoy any advantage until they could become quite large. If the first generation had been able to make itself just a little bit chubbier, it would have been all the more attractive to predators. Besides, the time and energy used for the swelling up, plus the loss of streamlining, would have been clear disadvantages for a creature trying to flee. Again, only the traits and abilities in their present form are advantageous for survival and thus natural selection. Anything less is clearly disadvantageous.

One might propose that the sea creatures' traits and abilities developed all at once from ordinary fish. But the scientific plausibility of such a proposal is on the level of that of fairy tales in which a table or other object suddenly becomes a horse at the flick of a wizard's wand or a frog becomes a prince when kissed by the princess.

Whether we like it or not, these fish can function only in their present state, with the many bodily features needed for the swelling and with the necessary complementary behavior. In other words, the defensive reactions and scare tactics of the puffer fish and spot-fin porcupine fish work only in their present form; the hypothetical intermediate variations are harmful mutations, not successful mutations pointing in the direction of further evolution, as evolutionists would have us believe.

Similarly interesting is the behavior of the short-horned lizard (*Phrynosoma douglasii*). This reptile, native to North America, can change its color from gray to brown and thus become virtually invisible against the desert sand. Sometimes it looks

just like a small rock. At night it digs a hole in the sand and rests, and during the day it crawls out of the hole to search for insects. In case its disguise fails and danger threatens, it swallows air, puffs itself up, and confronts the predator while jumping up and down and hissing. Snakes and other predators usually shun it because it has sharp spikes that would pierce their throat. But sometimes a reckless beast of prey takes a sudden fancy to lizard flesh and even the spikes do not scare it away. Then the short-horned lizard bursts a few veins in its eyes and shoots out a thin jet of blood from the corner of each eye toward its attacker—even as far as a yard! A well-aimed shot may temporarily blind the attacker, usually spoiling its appetite.

As with our previous cases, the short-horned lizard's unusual behavior is coupled with a very complex bodily construction. The problems with gradual evolutionary development of such features are the by-now familiar ones: the complex anatomical features (such as eyes capable of spurting blood), along with the complex behavioral patterns, are useful as a defense mechanism only in their complete form, not in their intermediary forms. And the sudden appearance of such complex biological systems, as if by magic, is completely impossible.

Collective defense

We should also mention the defense strategies of animals living in flocks or herds. Typically, members of a flock or herd will come together in a dense group to mislead the bird or beast of prey. This tactic makes

One wonders whether the blood-squirting method and the science of its application appeared merely by chance.

the predator's business more difficult, since it can only chase one selected member of the group and may thus lose sight of its prey in the crowd. Several species use this type of defense. Below we examine how starlings cluster together when they perceive a peregrine falcon.

Researchers of animal behavior use the term "key stimuli" to designate external phenomena that trigger a certain behavioral pattern in an animal. For starlings (*Sturnus vulgaris*) the shape of the peregrine falcon is a key stimulus. The shape of this bird of prey immediately sets off a reaction in the starlings' central nervous system, which results in the starlings' suddenly drawing close to one another and forming a dense flock. The peregrine falcon then cannot select a single target. As always, the question is how the starlings acquired this instinctual ability to identify the falcon's shape and then quickly flock together. The question is unanswerable from the evolutionist's point of view. The difficulty, as always, is that even

if some starlings somehow learned this effective response to the falcon, they could not have passed it on to their offspring, because acquired traits do not affect the genetic material. So it might be assumed that all previous generations of starlings behaved just like their current descendants.

From these examples it is clear that we will find in nature countless instances of complex defense mechanisms whose origin the theory of evolution is helpless to

On seeing a bird of prey, starlings instinctively cluster together to form a dense group.

explain. It seems much more reasonable to conclude that a being possessing higher intelligence equipped all species with the organs, knowledge, and abilities they need for defense.

Even so, we also see that even animals equipped with the best defense systems fall victim to predators from time to time. And ultimately, every living being dies. One may thus rightfully ask, "Why did this supposedly super-intelligent being design living beings with complex survival mechanisms but make them all ultimately succumb to death?" We will treat these philosophical questions in detail in the last chapter.

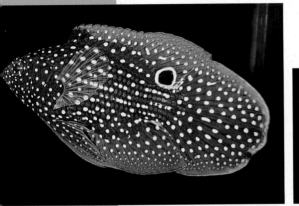

9

differences in the genetic material are due to arbitrary changes (mutations) in the deoxyribonucleic acid (DNA), which is responsible for the characteristics of living things. If such a trait proves to be advantageous in the given environment, the slightly different specimen and its issues have a better chance of surviving in the battle for life than other members of the same species. Those possessing less advantageous qualities slip into the background and gradually become extinct. Darwin termed this process *natural selection.* Incidental changes in the environment start another process of selection— again, better-fitted individuals survive and transmit their traits. According to this assumption, the form, size, and behavior of a species may completely change over the years. It is only a question of time before a one-celled being may "evolve" into such a complex being as, for example, man.

Counterarguments

This popular evolutionist view portrays the development of the living world as something like an amusing movie in which different plastic forms transform into one another in a spectacular way. But living things are much more refined and are far less malleable than plastic. It is questionable whether the basic physical features within a species can change enough to produce a new species. Observations in nature prove that the ability of living beings to adapt is limited. The breeding of domesticated animals for hundreds and even thousands of years has demonstrated that some traits of species (dogs, cats, cows, etc.) can be modified within certain limits—by conscious

selection. However, their basic characteristics do not change. Plant breeding has also shown that the extent of their transformability has limits. Breeders can modify size, shape, or color to some extent over several generations, but there is absolutely no way to produce a watermelon-sized plum or a pea-sized pear. Species can thus change within certain limits, but not without restraint. New organs and new structures never emerge in this way. Considering this, the theory, which assumes the possibility of both quantitatively and qualitatively infinite transformations, is rather bold, based on unsubstantiated "evidence." Darwinism, together with its modernized versions, is in fact an unfounded theory. Despite its relative popularity, many scientists seriously object to the theory of evolution; however, the public knows little or nothing of these objections.

The development of microbiology presents a new challenge to evolutionism. Darwin could not see into cells due to the undeveloped technology of microscopes in his day. Today, however, we know that even within a single cell-complex, cell organelles exist, displaying far-reaching relationships with, and incredibly complex biochemical processes between, one another. In fact, this cellular traffic is as regulated as the traffic of a major city. The extreme intricacy of these interrelated molecular systems and the fact that each of them presupposes the presence of other systems lead some preeminent scientists (among others, M. Behe, M. Denton, R. Thompson) to find it inconceivable that these "microscopic machines" could have developed in a gradual way.

We also find highly synchronized functioning in the organs of many animals. There

10

is no explanation as to how these allegedly "new" organs, which would have been useless in their developmental stages, appeared. According to the natural-selection view, only those traits survive that ensure a definite advantage for the living being in its survival. Most organs in their present form are completely suitable to fulfill their function. It is impossible to see how the very differently structured and functioning organs of the various classes of animals (fish, amphibians, reptiles, birds, mammals) could have transformed into another. Ceasing to function properly in the transformational stage, these new organs would have no tangible benefit for survival at every step. The evolutionary legend, which does not lack a touch of poetic quality, has no detailed rational scientific deduction. It is also worth considering that most organs of the body do not function separately, but in concordance with other organs or systems of organs. If one of them changes, the other related systems should also change simultaneously. This is very hard to conceive if one supposes only random changes.

In the field of paleontology, evolutionists have historically faced the problem that in ancient layers of earth there is no trace of any series of transformational forms from one species to another. From time to time, they label a series of fossils arbitrarily put together as an "evolutionary chain." There is no proof, however, that the given entities actually evolved from one another; rather it appears they are instead a separate species with no genealogical relationship. On the contrary, there is archeological evidence showing that certain species looked exactly the same tens of millions of years ago as they do today. Emerging fossils are often put into an "evolutionary order" based merely on evolutionary preconceptions, and anomalous evidence is ignored. Current scientific books (such as *Forbidden Archeology* by Michael A. Cremo and Richard L. Thompson) have exposed this process of manipulating facts.

The secret of the instincts

In light of this information, the theory of evolution is bleeding from many wounds, being attacked on several weak points. Each objection raised against it would deserve a separate volume. In our present book we mainly explore the origin of animal instincts, which is a rather unexplained field of biology. Instincts and instinctive behaviors are still more or less quite a mystery. Among the disciplines, the science of animal behavior, or ethology, deals with mapping the natural behavior and habits of animals. Thanks to extensive research in this field, we know the behavioral patterns of many animal species quite well. Charles Darwin compared the behavior and emotions of different living beings with one another, and he sought to explain them within the framework of his own phylogenetic theory.

Researchers specializing in this field, like Konrad Lorenz and Nikolas Tinbergen, also tried to interpret the different phenomena of the living world based on the theory of evolution. With the help of their comparative studies they managed to separate hereditary and learned (i.e. acquired) elements of behavior from one another.

According to the presently accepted explanation, the source of hereditary traits is

Partnerships

Partnerships

Having examined different feeding interactions, let us now turn to other relationships between species. In the following sections we first present various ways that organisms coexist to their mutual benefit. Then we explore some cases in which the relationship harms one of the partners—even fatally. Could nature's blind processes of accidental mutation and natural selection have produced these curious relationships, or were the participants destined for each other from the outset?

Do the big fish eat the little fish?

Whether living on the land, in the sea, or in the air, organisms are almost always troubled by smaller creatures known as parasites. These generally tiny animals sneak uninvited into their host through the skin, mouth, intestines, or respiratory system and cause the host much trouble. The suffering party is naturally very pleased if someone comes to relieve it of the unwanted guests. But if the animal tormented by parasites is a formidable predator, this task is far from easy.

Let us take an excursion into the fabulous world of coral reefs, where millions of plants and animals live side by side. Though superficially a sea paradise, in truth the world of coral reefs is a terrifying place for its occupants, for behind any coral outcropping could lurk a hungry predator. The smaller fish have to be alert at all times. When, for instance, a goliath grouper (*Epinephelus itajara*) swims up from the depths, panic breaks out among the smaller creatures and they flee in all directions—except for a slender little fish that dances forward boldly from its hiding place, thumbing its

nose at approaching death. And what's more, it swims *toward* the grouper! Has this fish lost its senses? Why hasn't the survival instinct prompted it to flee with all the other fish?

The little fish is the blue-streak cleaner wrasse (*Labroides dimidiatus*), of the blenny family. We might think it will soon disappear into the grouper's stomach once and for all, but if we continue watching we'll see some surprising events. The goliath grouper suddenly stops, completely opens its gills, and waits motionless, with jaws wide open. Then the cleaner wrasse courageously swims into the grouper's mouth and starts to bite off parasites and remove dead skin. The sanguinary predator bears the often-painful cleaning process with patience while it carefully avoids harming the diligent little fish. When the cleaner wrasse finishes its business, it triumphantly swims out of the huge mouth, and the grouper leaves satisfied. Though it doesn't tip its small benefactor, it does allow it to live and eat its fill while cleaning. Sometimes two or three

wrasses work on a grouper at once, like mechanics changing a wheel on a Formula 1 racing car at a pit stop. Even though the cleaner wrasses are quite efficient (in six hours they can attend to as many as three hundred groupers), the "patients" waiting for treatment often line up in long queues. There are several species of cleaner fish. The blue-head cleaner wrasse (*Thalassoma bifasciatum*) also feeds on the epidermic parasites of bigger fish. Each variety of cleaner wrasse opens its office within a given territory, and the bigger fish wishing treatment visit these places.

The goliath grouper is not a particularly friendly sight for a small fish. Still, the bluestreak cleaner wrasse dances confidently in front of its mouth.

The blue-streak cleaner wrasse swims into the mouth of the grouper. Both of them benefit, but how does the small fish know that it has nothing to fear? How does the goliath grouper know that it should not harm this particular small fish?

Spared escorts

If we leave the coral reefs and head out to sea, we will find a species of cleaner called pilot fish that treat the most dangerous of predators—sharks. In the kingdom of sharks,

pilot fish (*Naucrates ductor*) live an adventurous life. This species, with its distinctive dark vertical stripes, likes warm seas. These fish have gotten their name because they escort ships, whales, manta rays, and sharks. Divers unanimously report that sharks rarely swim without the striped pilot fish. A shark is usually joined by a dozen or so, and the dangerous predator moves forward majestically with its retinue. We do not know whether pilot fish are aware of how dangerous sharks are. In any case, they crowd around it in a carefree manner without the slightest sign of fear, and the shark makes no attempt to catch them. This is all the more startling because the beast has an insatiable appetite and is not picky about its food. What's more, like the aforementioned cleaner wrasses, pilot fish will often fearlessly enter a shark's mouth and clean fragments of food from between its teeth.

Another reason why sharks regard pilot fish as friends is that the pilots always notice pieces of dead flesh floating in the water, which they indicate to the shark with zigzag movements. Many sailors have reported that pilot fish will sample the flesh

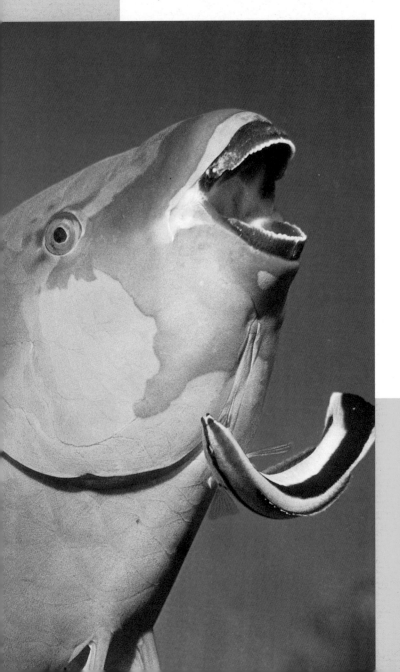

The parrot fish also asks for an appointment to have a small "dental treatment" in the bluestreak cleaner wrasse's office.

Moray eels are dangerous predators, but they leave the cleaner wrasse alone. How do they know that this small fish is different from others?

and call the sharks only if it proves edible. It has recently been discovered that from time to time pilot fish will also remove parasites from a shark's body.

Pilot fish are not averse to looking after rays either. The manta ray (*Manta birostris*) invitingly opens wide its huge mouth, into which the pilot fish swim without the least fear and clean off unwanted guests. Sea biologists report that when pilot fish have to flee, they like to hide in the mouth of a nearby ray, where they are completely safe. As with its prey, the ray drives the pilot fish into its mouth with two spade-shaped appendices on its head, but it never swallows the pilots.

Cleaner wrasses and pilot fish feel perfectly safe around the dangerous predators they consort with. A researcher examined the stomach of several hundred predator fish but found no cleaner wrasses in any of them. And the same holds for the pilot fish. Sharks are voracious—they devour everything in their path. That's why fishermen and sailors like to open the stomachs of dead sharks: there's a chance they contain something valuable. But no remnants of pilot fish have ever been

found in a shark's stomach. In other words, sharks swallow up practically everything—except pilot fish! The shark is like a wily businessman who has signed a contract with the pilot fish: "I won't eat you, and you'll clean my teeth and guide me to food. It's a deal."

The date of the contract?

The symbiosis between various cleaner fish and predators gives rise to the following question: How could these astonishing relationships have begun? The smaller party (the pilot fish or the cleaner wrasse) enjoy the benefit of protection in both cases, plus they get plenty of food. On the other hand, the predator fish rid themselves of unwanted parasites and, in the case of the pilot fish, have an easier time finding food. But how did the two parties develop this

45

The small cleaner wrasse clears away dermal parasites at the dorsal fin of the surgeonfish.

46

business? Evolution's attempt to explain it confronts serious difficulties.

Modern evolution theory would assume that the ancestors of the cleaner wrasses fed in the traditional way, i.e., by consuming small creatures stuck to the sea bottom or rocks. And if the wrasses sensed an approaching predator, they fled quickly, driven by their survival instinct, and disappeared in a hiding place. Then one day, say the evolutionists, a mutation occurred that changed a wrass's instinctual behavior: instead of feeding in the normal way, it swam toward its mortal enemy—a goliath grouper, for example—blithely entered its mouth, and began to eat its fill of the parasites in the big fish's mouth. (The same scenario would hold for the pilot fish vis-à-vis sharks.)

This scenario is completely inconceivable. The theory of evolution states that in the constant struggle for survival small fish that swim fastest and find the best hiding place from predators will survive and propagate. Conversely, predator fish survive and propagate when they are the best at pursuing and catching their prey. It would be suicidal for one proto–cleaner-fish, as a result of some genetically induced mental quirk, to suddenly reverse this instinctual behavior and approach its natural predator unless the predator itself had the corresponding idea of accommodating the cleaner in its mouth. So, what are the chances that the one mutant proto–cleaner-fish out of countless millions of ordinary fish would meet up with the one mutant grouper or

The hermit crab sometimes places cnidarians on the shell it drags along with it. Since cnidarians have a poisonous bite, they keep away predators. Did the hermit crab discover this, or is it acting according to the direction of an intelligent creator? (The cnidarians also benefit from the affair: they feed on the remnants of the crab's meals.)

shark ready to welcome it instead of swallow it up? Zero. Thus it is nonsensical to suggest that, because of chance mutation, a small fish would suddenly approach a predator without inhibitions with the idea of getting food from its mouth, while simultaneously the predator would welcome the little fish, its natural prey, with the understanding that the little fish would relieve the predator of annoying parasites, and that the former predator and prey would then propagate generations of fish that continued this symbiotic relationship. Such stories are fit for storybooks, not scientific literature.

Neither logic nor our knowledge of biology supports the theory of a gradual evolution of mutually beneficial symbiosis between members of different species. It is much more reasonable to conclude that these "couples" appeared together, meant for each other from the outset. From the very first moment of their existence, they instinctively acted in such a way as to further the symbiotic relationship. The small fish knew exactly which predator they needn't fear, and the corresponding predator knew which little fish to accommodate in return for their sanitation or guidance services. This cooperation between species can be successful only if both parties know their function and play the appropriate role on the big stage of life. We can rightfully conclude that the symbiotic couples are actors in a play written by a higher intelligence; the instructions of the author strictly determine the characteristics of the actors and their relationship to the other participants.

Land partners

Many pairs of land creatures also display remarkable partnerships. The colorful Egyptian plover (*Pluvianus aegyptius*) lives by the banks of African inland waters, sharing its habitat with the Nile crocodile. One can easily recognize this thrush-sized bird of the pratincole family by its yellow vest, black-and-white-striped head, and gray-blue wings. It is bound to the crocodile in a strange alliance. The plover uses its shrill call to inform the crocodile of every movement in the environment. This call helps the reptile because it usually indicates the presence of prey. The crocodile has no fear of enemies since it has none, and in the person of the bird—to use the expression of a Russian researcher—even the crocodile has a friend.

We should note that the Nile crocodile is not particularly picky about its food: it eats fish, birds, mammals (unfortunately even humans on occasion), and even smaller crocodiles. It is thus rather surprising that the Egyptian plover walks undisturbed among the crocodiles, plucking leeches and other parasites from their skin. In this way the bird gets food and the crocodile is relieved of some inconveniences.

The plover-crocodile symbiosis resembles our marine examples in several

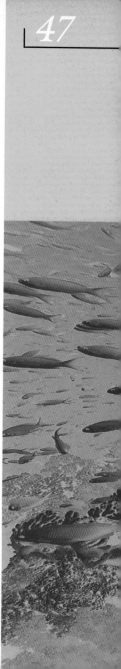

respects—and similar questions arise about the origin of this advantageous alliance. Why would an ancestor of the plover have tried to make friends with the crocodile, when every other animal in Africa instinctively avoids it as much as possible? And even if a naive plover had approached it, the crocodile would certainly have fixed its recklessness once and for all. Consequently, this reptile-bird relationship could not have evolved by chance mutations either. The most plausible explanation is that the two parties appeared together, as permanent actors in a play better staged than a Shakespearean drama.

The Egyptian plover is not afraid of the crocodile; it feeds on parasites living in the crocodile's skin.

Friendships are made in heaven. The Egyptian plover approaches the crocodile despite its fearful sight.

No rose without a thorn

Let us now return to the depths of the sea. As the beautiful sight of the coral reefs again unfolds before us, we notice a strange little fish. Its body bears distinctive bright-orange

stripes alternating with white ones, and its fins are dark-edged. Known as the common clownfish (*Amphiprion percula*), this tiny denizen of the sea lives in close symbiosis with the sea anemone, whose poison is lethal. Sea anemones (*Actinaria*) kill their victims with venomous stings from the nematocysts at the tips of their tentacles. But the colorful clownfish is immune. Constantly swimming carefree among the anemone's tentacles, it lives in the latter's embrace. Predatory fish, however, carefully avoid the sea anemone because they know the strength of its deadly poison. In the shelter of the sea anemone, the clownfish doesn't have to hide among the coral reefs when a predator appears; it is completely safe and can simply swim about undisturbed.

But how does the sea anemone benefit from this relationship? Scientists who first

Fair's fair. African buffalos are relieved from their parasites by oxpeckers, who in turn get their food. The otherwise quite irritable animals peacefully tolerate the presence of the industrious birds.

The cattle egret chose the hippopotamus as its place of resting.

49

The clownfish has a special chemical covering that protects it from the deadly poison of the sea anemone.

cles. When a butterfly fish appears, the clownfish immediately stands up for its friend and chases away the attacker. Sea anemone and clown fish: a perfect match.

For a long time biologists did not understand why sea anemones do not catch and kill clownfish. Then trials carried out in coral reefs off the Niccobar Islands solved the puzzle. Researchers observed that when a clownfish approaches a sea anemone for the first time in its life, it is very careful: it brushes against only one or two tentacles and then swims away. With time the clownfish becomes increasingly bold, until finally it swims about with abandon amid the anemone's mortally dangerous arms. When a scientist took a young clownfish who had had no previous contact with

observed this symbiosis thought the anemone must benefit in some way, since it appeared to appreciate the little fish very much. Experiments proved this hypothesis correct. Researchers placed a sea anemone in an aquarium with many fish, but no clownfish. The lonely anemone remained rather colorless, with half-withdrawn tentacles. But when a clownfish was put into the water, the anemone soon made friends with it; gradually the anemone attained its normal color and, opening its ring of tentacles, slowly emerged from lassitude. The reason is that the clownfish's constant swimming about enables the anemone to get lots of fresh water and bits of food. Also, the clownfish protects the sea anemone from its enemy, the butterfly fish (*Blennius sp.*). This fish is also immune to the anemone's poison and likes to clip its tenta-

50

anemones and pressed it against the anemone's tentacles, the fish instantly died from the poison. But when the scientist did the same with adult specimens, nothing happened. However, when he scraped off the thin gelatinous layer from the adults' skin and put them back into contact with the sea anemone, they died instantly.

The secret was thus revealed: the clownfish are covered with a gelatinous layer that protects them from the anemone's nematocysts. Young clownfish do not have this chemical coating, since it develops only after they first touch the sea anemone and a few nematocysts pierce the fish's skin. This is why young clownfish are so prudent at first. With the help of the nematocysts, the clownfish "vaccinates" itself against the poison. Researchers therefore concluded that the clownfish's system of defense includes hereditary behavior (the cautious first approach) and a genetically coded protective layer whose development is triggered by the first encounter.

Once again the theory of evolution totally fails to explain the origin of this symbiotic relationship. In vain would an ancestor of the clownfish have decided to retire into the shelter of the sea anemone since without a protective layer it would have instantly perished. Or perhaps once in millions of years, one day a mutant fish was born with the possibility to grow a chemical

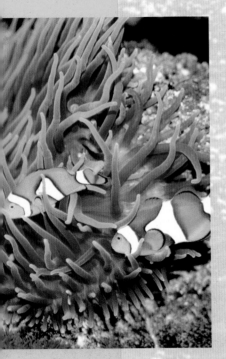

The clownfish provokes admiration more than laughter from the spectator when the sea anemones are involved.

protective layer. It would not have derived much benefit from it, because how would it have known that it had this new ability? And if it had somehow gotten among the arms of the sea anemone, sadly enough, it would have died since it had not "vaccinated" itself with due precaution; consequently the chemical armor could not have developed. It would have expired in this case, too, just as the theory of evolution expires amid these very lines of print.

It seems to be out of the question that the mutant little fish would have learned how to approach the sea anemone and how to grow the protective layer on its body. The possibility of learning is further diminished by the fact that it can take a chance only once. Inventiveness is no explanation either because learned characteristics or behaviors are not transmitted into the genes. But the

The clownfish swims boldly into the tentacles of the sea anemone because it knows that what is danger for others is protection for it. Their strange relationship cannot be the product of evolution. Either it is immune from, and therefore protected from, the poison—or not; there are no intermediary stages.

clownfish's behavior (the way it cautiously approaches the sea anemone) is hereditary and congenital.

The sea anemone and the clownfish are also actors in the ancient drama of the world, actors whose sensational performances were scripted by a skilled playwright. He was the one who implanted the appropriate patterns of behavior into the players of the spectacle, and they have been presenting this show successfully on nature's stage for a long time.

Paid mercenaries

We again set foot on shore, waving goodbye to the mysterious coral reefs of the sea, and head for the jungle, in the heart of which we may discover similar phenomena. We will see that in these relationships, one party protects while the other "pays" its bodyguard for the safety gained this way.

While we roam the wilderness, we notice ants carrying leaves. The Australian weaver ants stitch their nest together from leaves, and for this operation, they use their young's discharge as glue.

The weaver ants (Oecophylla) feed on caterpillars. However, there is one caterpillar that does not dread them—in fact it gets along quite well with them. The back of the caterpillar known as the centaur oakblue (*Arhopala centaurus*) is full of tiny warts that, when irritated, excrete a sweetish, sugary fluid. This caterpillar has other tiny glands, too, which produce amino acids. The weaver ants are most fond of these two substances. Therefore, instead of tearing the

52

caterpillar apart, they look after it with solicitous care and even build a small night shelter for it. In the morning when it sets out to get food, they follow it like a mercenary army, guarding it every step of the way. If a predator—a wasp or a spider—attacks it, they spurt formic acid on the attacker to protect their protégé. In return for their service, they "milk" the caterpillar by patting it to stimulate the excretion of sweet fluid; they also scratch off amino-acidic pieces of tissue from its skin.

It seems the ants are thoroughly exploiting the caterpillar, just as farmers exploit their cows. But the caterpillar also benefits. If it reaches a tree where there are no ants, a predator will soon devour it. In a trial aimed at assessing this danger, none of several hundred caterpillars survived. Is the caterpillar only a passive beneficiary of the hospitality of the ants, or is it active in creating the partnership? The answer lies in one of its anatomical features. On the back of the caterpillar, there are two small feather-like organs. When spread out, they emit a scent. Moreover, they emit a soft buzzing sound; if you put the caterpillar on your finger, you can feel a vibration from this. Both signals attract the ants' attention. The smell and the sound indicate that the ants should pet this caterpillar rather than eat it. Thus we cannot consider the caterpillar to be just like a cow forced to yield milk. It is more appropriate to compare it to a sovereign who maintains a well-armed military in return for payment.

Let us begin the analysis of the special relationship between the weaver ants and the centaur oakblue caterpillars in relation to the origin of insects. Evolutionists only guess about the origin of insects and Articulata in general. Having several million species, Articulata is the largest animal genus. The segmental structure of their body is unique, but at the same time, their senses and nervous system are highly developed. The fact that their anatomical structure differs from all other animals makes their origin unexplainable. Because annelids most resemble insects in their segmental structure, some scientists postulate Articulata evolved from annelids. However, there is obviously much difference between an earthworm and a dragonfly. This is most likely the reason many evolutionists do not agree with this theory. But they cannot suggest a resolution.

The zephyr blue caterpillar lives in symbiosis with ants that lick the sweet liquid secreted by it.

the symbiosis of these two creatures is more likely to have existed since their beginning. If the caterpillar evolved from another being, its ancestor would have had to possess a defense system against predators. As it developed its current defense mechanism, it would have gradually given up its old one. But we see that today it can only survive with the help of complex organs (e.g., the small membranes on its back), the gradual development of which would have required considerable time. According to the principle of selection, only the most apt and most able organisms survive. Certainly the oakblue caterpillar, undergoing such a process of change, would have got caught in the selection filter. Their survival would be comparable to successfully transforming a propeller airplane into a supersonic jet while airborne by gradually dismantling one system and simultaneously building up the other. It is impossible even in theory.

For the sake of argument, let's suppose the impossible: by a magic mutation, a perfect wonder, the centaur oakblue caterpillar appeared in its present form as the issue of an ancestor totally different from it. The weaver ants would have no concept of its existence; therefore, they would take no notice of the scent and sound signals emitted by it. And if they had accidentally bumped into each other in the forest, the ants would have ruthlessly torn the novel caterpillar apart. Thus, we can hardly consider their relationship the result of an evolutionary process. The team of centaur oakblue caterpillars and weaver ants appears to pin the great Darwin's theory to the ground.

Despite this puzzlement and the lack of theoretical support and archeological evidence, the accepted view taught in schools is Articulata are a product of evolution. The questions, "Where do they come from?" and "How did they evolve?" are still unanswered. Perhaps the answers are not within the confines of the theory of evolution.

The relationship between the centaur oakblue caterpillar and the weaver ants supports the view that representatives of the insect world did not evolve from one another or from simpler ancestors, but were created the way they are today. Experiments have shown that the caterpillar is unable to stay alive without the ants. Thus

The moth and the anthill

We now focus on animals that take advantage of other living beings. Parasitic moths are rare, yet a few species plague other beings to death. The Australian weaver ants just mentioned also coexist with the caterpillar of a relative of the centaur oakblue, the amaryllis azure (*Ogyris amaryllis*). This insect, contrary to the centaur oakblue caterpillar, does not have soft skin nor does it produce any sweet fluid. Rather, an oval brown shield covers its body from the end of its abdomen to its ears. This caterpillar does not at all resemble a peaceful cow, nor even an obese sovereign, but rather an enemy tank.

The weird creature penetrates into the weaver ants' nest and, while it slowly creeps forward on the leaf, it presses down the edges of its back shield so that the ants cannot wedge themselves under it and attack its soft parts. Their mandibles glance off the smooth chitin surface. The caterpillar pushes itself forward until it reaches the ant larvae within the leaf nest. Then it suddenly lifts its shield while still marching and lets it down again, trapping the closest unfortunate larva. Then, safe in its impenetrable shelter, the caterpillar slowly and comfortably chews its prey. The intruder caterpillar does not leave the anthill and subsists this way until it is fully developed. The ants can do nothing against it; they can neither render it harmless, nor throw it out. The caterpillar enters into the pupa state there, and the fully developed moth hatches among the ants.

We might think that after the moth hatches the time of revenge comes for the ants. Quite surprisingly, however, the hatching moth, though no longer having a shield, is also immune from the ants' attack! The reason is that the moth is entirely covered (even its wings) with very fine, loose scales. If the ants attack it, the scales peel off from it, obstructing the ants' mandibles and tentacles while the moth escapes pursuit and emerges into the world.

This moth species applies very tricky and sophisticated techniques. Could the amaryllis azure and its special caterpillar form have evolved through gradual changes? Gradual

The caterpillar of the amaryllis azure intrudes into an anthill like a tank. By lifting its shield, it captures a larva from time to time and devours it. Its "armor" serves its purpose only in its caterpillar form.

54

Parasitic species are equipped with specialized sense organs and apparatuses that allow them to find and exploit their host animals (or humans) by tuning in to them.

development of the defense shield and the scales on the hatching moth is inconceivable. A caterpillar with "half-ready" armor would be unable to survive the attack of the ants. The defense system is useful only in its complete form. It is difficult, if not impossible, to imagine that these features could have appeared all at once, in complete harmony, from a different moth species. If they could not evolve gradually or suddenly transform from a different species, we must consider another explanation. It is much more logical to conclude that these moths initially entered this world fully equipped with the means of self-protection and knowledge necessary for their survival.

The double parasite

Finally, let us examine the reproductive technique of the South American warble fly. The larvae of many bloodsucking insects develop in the host animal, feeding on its tissues. Warble flies are such insects. Their host is a mammal, usually a hoofed animal. The South American warble fly, instead of putting its eggs directly in the host animal, catches a bloodsucking fly and puts its eggs on the abdomen of the latter! The fly then transports the larvae of the warble fly to its next victim without even knowing it. While they suck blood, the warble fly larvae quickly hatch out from the eggs and drive themselves into the skin of the host animal. In this way, the warble fly not only lives off other animals, it exploits another parasite by having its larvae transported to their destination by a colleague, the bloodsucking fly!

A thought-provoking question in this case is, "Why would a 'primitive' warble fly, one that puts its eggs in the usual way into the body of a host animal, use the service of another insect?" This method does not seem to be a whit more advantageous from the point of view of successful survival. It rather intimates a playful intelligence that is willing to apply unusual methods (requiring the intervention of other species) in determining its mode of reproduction.

In this chapter we examined a few basic types of closely coexisting animal species. We have seen examples of both self-imposed and forced modes of coexistence. The relationship between life partners can be harmonious but also rather unpleasant for one of them. But we can see that species connected to each other are perfectly adjusted in their behavior as well as in their anatomy. Blind chance does not account for this harmony. It is more probable that a higher intelligence with creative imagination arranged these perennial pairs. We will return later to the question, "What made such a higher intelligence do this?"

56

The language
of the animals

The Language of the Animals

Animals communicate in many ways: by sounds or visible signs, or even by transmission of chemicals and electric stimuli. On the following pages, we provide examples from both sides of communication: the emitting organs and functions, and the apparatus of reception, as well as the process of information exchange (the topic of bio-communication connected to courting and race preservation will be explored in a later chapter). We also address the highly implausible theory that complex forms of animal communication came into being by gradual evolution. At this point, theories of evolution cannot reasonably explain these phenomena, while the theory of intelligent design can.

58

Scent Messages

Except for birds, all animal groups use chemical substances called pheromones to communicate. Various scents are used for various purposes. There are scents that attract attention, scents that frighten enemies, scents that help one animal find another, and scents that facilitate sexual life or care of the young.

Let's examine how an apparently simple being, the ant (*Formicoidea*), uses scents to communicate. We'll start with a short description of a few kinds of ant colonies.

Scientists have found more than eleven thousand ant species. Each species lives its coordinated, splendidly organized life in a nest. Ants have varying shapes and sizes according to the functions they assume. Workers are wingless, sexually undeveloped females with huge mandibles. They are the ones who take care of the eggs, larvae, and pupae. They also forage for food, keep the nest clean—in brief, they do nest service. Soldier ants, also female, have sword-like mandibles to fend off or attack enemies by stinging or biting. The only thing males do is

fertilize the females; shortly afterward they die. The queens' sole job is to lay eggs. In one nest, several queens may get along with each other (unlike bees, where there is only one queen). Not all these forms are present in each species, but females, males and workers are always needed.

The fine nuances of social function found in the "caste system" of ants cannot be found even in vertebrate species, except for humans! Ants of the same species who perform these varied functions often differ so much in appearance, size, and bodily structure that they appear to belong to totally different species. They differ from one another more than a mouse differs from a guinea pig or a sparrow from a crow. How is it possible that from eggs laid by the same queen such startlingly different brothers and sisters can emerge?

What causes these extreme modifications within one species?

Scientific research has revealed that queen ants have a system of exocrine glands that influence the life of the nest. Pheromones, the volatile substances excreted by these glands, have specific stimulating or inhibiting effects on the inhabitants of the nest, especially on developing larvae. For instance, a certain pheromone inhibits the development of sexual organs in females; thus they remain sterile and assume the role of workers. This pheromone is excreted on the surface of the queen's body, and female workers imbibe it by licking her. Then they transmit it to the whole colony.

Pheromones also play a vital role in communication within the ant colony. Various pheromones have different scents, which the ants perceive with an olfactory organ on their

Red wood ants inform each other about the location of food by chemical communication.

The larvae of the army ants produce pheromones that keep the trail in motion. When they enter the pupa state, they cease to emit messages and thus the army settles down. The whole process is very well thought out!

The organized life of the anthill is possible due to a perfect communication system.

60

antennae. Ants use more than thirty phero-mones in their social life, the functions of some of which remain to be determined. But we do know that ants have more than ten glands from which some pheromones get to their bodily surface, others to their oral cavity, and yet others to the hole at the rear of their body. Certain tropical ants have glands on their feet, enabling them to leave scented footprints that form a track leading to food. Some ant species leave a strong scent track to an abundant food source and a weak one to a meager source. This is how the news spreads so quickly to our local ant colony when we leave a jar of honey on the pantry shelf with honey dribbling on the outside. In general, pheromones provide an efficient way for members of the same ant species to make their way home after finding a food source and telling their friends of the treasure.

Besides this elaborate system of chemical communication, the ants also communicate through physical stimuli. For example, they will transmit signals to each other by touching antennae. They can communicate more than thirty signs to each other this way.

Certain ant species exhibit special habits and abilities along with the necessary system of communication. For example, South Ame-rican army ants (*Eciton hamatum*) march in extremely long columns in search of food. Hunters march at the head, while behind them workers carrying larvae march in a long line, protected on both sides by an army of blind soldiers with huge mandibles. When the hunters find some prey, they overrun it and cut it to pieces. Meanwhile, the larvae are producing pheromones that keep the march in motion by spreading among the lines of the army. When the larvae pupate they cease to emit pheromones, and the army settles down.

Then the workers start an astounding operation: they cling to each other and with their own bodies form a nest, or bivouac, in which they create corridors for the queen and closets for the pupae. The queen lays eggs, and from the pupae the new generation comes out and excretes the substances stimulating a migration—and the troop sets out on a new march.

Southeast Asian weaver ants (*Oecophylla*) build their nests from stitched-together leaves, but their means of stitching is extraordinary. A troop of workers will join two leaves by holding one with their mandibles and the other with their feet. Meanwhile, fellow workers stitch the leaves together on the other side by dragging young larvae and squeezing them gently between their mandibles—because the larvae produce silk! At the leaf joints, the ants carry the living tubular glue-pots to and fro until the silky mess unites the edges of the leaves.

Honeypot ants (*Myrmecocystus*) live in dry regions of North America and Australia, and are famous for their clever food-storing method. In

times of plenty, they forcefully feed so much nectar to members of a special caste of workers that their uniquely structured abdomens swell to the size of peas and become transparent. Other workers then lift these "honeypots" to the ceiling of the nest so they can hang there. When food is scarce, the living honeypots squeeze small portions of food out of their mouths upon request.

Leafcutter ants (*Atta sp.*) maintain a mushroom bed and feed on the fruit of the mushrooms. The bed of the mushrooms is made of leaves. The ants cut out pieces of leaves with their mandibles and lift them on their back like sails to drag them inside the anthill. The pieces of leaves are broken into smaller pieces and

mixed with saliva by the workers. The finely cut leaves are then spread over the mushroom bed or used to start new cultures.

In the previous chapter, we discussed the weaver ants that live inseparably with caterpillars in a mutually advantageous relationship. There is an inter-species communication when vibrations of the "featherlets" on the caterpillars' backs are detected and decoded by the ants, just as radar detects acoustic waves.

Certain ant species keep aphides as "milk cows." The photo shows the mother aphis and the small aphides with an ant.

62

If you can't do it yourself... Ants leave an odor track so fellow ants can find the prey.

Ants belonging to the genus of *Lasius* are active animal breeders. Yellow meadow ants (*Lasius flavus*), for example, keep aphids as "milk cows." They eat the aphids' liquid feces of high sugar content, the so-called honeydew, and in return, they protect them and take care of them. In case of danger, they carry their "domestic animals" with them.

Slaveholder Amazon ants (*Polyergus rufescens*) also behave in an unusual way. They attack the anthill of another ant species and drag away their pupas. Amazon ants have mandibles so huge that they are unable to take food independently. They can stay alive only if the slaves coming out of the pupas feed them.

Remember that in each of these ant societies a communication system that suits their greatly differing modes of behavior is required. There is no scientific explanation based on evolutionary theory for any of these communication systems, not to mention a detailed account of how each species developed step by step from certain other species. Yet scientific reasoning should be able to fulfill this requirement. The superficial explanations of evolutionists create more questions than they answer.

Impossible mission

Let us consider this problem further. There are many more special types of ant societies than those previously described. They all have one thing in common: all members of a specific species or anthill behave in a way that is

characteristic of their species, serving common goals in perfect harmony with all other members of the same species. The communication by each individual also serves the purpose of effective cooperation. Each group or individual has to know and execute its task perfectly to ensure the survival of the entire anthill.

It is a fact that insect societies function almost perfectly; each individual behaves exactly as is required for the interests of the community. It is obvious, however, that these tiny creatures are not aware of the practicality of their actions. Each act is a result of instincts and innate reactions to stimuli and signals, not of "knowledge" in the human sense.

This raises a few perplexing questions in connection with the origin of ant "cultures."

The central problem is the diverse anatomical structures, behaviors, and ways of communication of different ant species. The physical features of each species—and within the species, of the different groups assuming different tasks—are perfectly suitable to carry out the specific activities for which they are used. Note, for example, the formidable mandibles of the army ants, the swelling abdomen of the honeypot ants, and the system of glands facilitating the commu-

nication of all ant species. Furthermore, these constitutional abilities coincide perfectly with the suitable models of behavior. According to the theory of evolution, these species supposedly evolved by "adapting" themselves to circumstances, i.e., by "modifying" their body and behavior according to environmental requirements. Such statements are not at all scientific. Those of this opinion must also account for how and from what these special ant species and organs have evolved. Without such an explanation, the evolutionary view is an unfounded system of beliefs.

We have mentioned, for example, the mushroom-growing ants. These ants carry pieces of leaf into their anthill where they cut them into even finer pieces. Then they thoroughly chew them to use them as substrate for their food, the mushrooms. How and from what species could this behavior have evolved? Naturally, they came from a species (evolutionists would say) that did not yet grow mushrooms or cut leaves, because neither was edible for them. According to the usual explanation, evolutionary changes occur through mutations—small genetic modifications—step by step, over a long time. However, it is inconceivable that such minute, incidental steps could have created the

present complex social behavior and accompanying system of information exchange.

Consider the main elements required for the present behavior. The ants have to have mandibles suitable for cutting leaves; they have to know that their business is to carry pieces of inedible leaves into the anthill; they have to know that once in the anthill, they have to chew and spread the substrate. In addition to all this, they have to have an appropriate system of communication to be able to carry out their mass operations (they can completely rob a tree of its foliage in a single day). Furthermore, it is very interesting that before her mating flight, the future queen puts a bit of the home mushroom crop in her buccal pocket and leaves the anthill with it. In her new hole, she begins to nurse this culture, which will then serve the sustenance of the new anthill. The queen also has to have the instinct that ensures that she does not "forget" to take the future pantry of the new empire with her.

For leafcutter ants to successfully stay alive and function, all these factors are required simultaneously, in perfect harmony. Therefore, it is not possible that they have come into existence by evolution.

Further complicating this picture is the fact that even within a single ant species, there are often several types of groups with completely different bodily structures and tasks. These, however, are constituent parts of the anthill that are mutually dependent on one another; their different activities are connected like cogwheels in a clock. It is thus inconceivable that the interdependent mutations of these different groups could come into being by chance, independent from each other, and still perfectly support each other's activities.

Similarly mysterious is the communication of these specially behaving species: they all have the appropriate organs and glands able to receive and emit scent marks. They are born with the ability to know how to react to each scent. In other words, the supposed evolutionist explanation (still nonexistent) should be able to account for the anatomical changes and the accompanying behavioral modifications, the concerted transformation of the overall behaviors of the different groups, and the simultaneous change in the communication system. We invite our more skeptical readers to try to explain the creation of any of the previously mentioned ant societies in this way, remembering that the imaginary process should in each case consist of small steps advantageous for the species.

We consider this intellectual effort a logically fruitless attempt. We are convinced that one who wants to solve the mystery of how different animal behaviors and communication systems came into existence by evolution undertakes an inextricable task.

One more thought-provoking note: ant fossils have been discovered in tertiary layers (sixty million years old). These ancient ants belonged to the same genera that we know today. From this, researchers concluded that the structure of their society must have been very similar to that of the present forms. In other words, ants have not changed.

We have sufficient theoretical and experimental basis to suppose that the present forms of ants' social behavior and chemical-based information exchange are not the result of their transformation from another animal group. It is much more probable that characteristic traits of all ant species have survived and been transmitted unchanged through time. The physical structure of these tiny creatures, their cooperative and effective behavior, and their network of social relations all indicate the existence of an infinitely great and supremely intelligent being.

Swimming power plants

Manmade water-powered electric plants are able to ensure the power supply of entire cities. Humanity, thanks to Italian physicist Alessandro Volta, has known how to produce electricity since 1800. But in nature, electricity has existed for much longer.

Certain fish, for example, are able to generate electricity. The electric ray (*Torpedo torpedo*), the elephantphis (*Gnathonemus ibis*) living in the Nile, the electric catfish (*Malapterurus electricus*), and the electric eel

(*Electrophorus electricus*) are such fish species.

The structure of the organ generating the electricity is similar to a battery. The above-mentioned animals are also able to perceive electricity with the aid of special receptors connected to their lateral line. One of the ways they use the current generated is by creating an electric field around themselves. If an unknown animal breaches it, they are able to perceive it due to the modifications of the field's lines of force. Another benefit of the generation of the current is that by electric shock, they can numb or even kill a prey animal and then eat it.

The electric eel, measuring more than eight feet long, lives in fresh water in South America. Its current-generating organ, which extends to four-fifths the length of its body, has several functions. The organ consists of a series of small, low-voltage electrode plates. The animal is able to compound the voltage of all the plates to emit an electric discharge as strong as 500 volts. This would make even a mule collapse! This fish, living in turbulent, muddy waters, is weak sighted and hunts with the help of electricity. The electricity can also spread in water as a signal and transmit information to fellow members of the same species. This is electronic communication par excellence, although not as sophisticated as television or the Internet. Electric eels identify each other with the help of these signals. They distinguish the stronger, more frequent electric signals emitted by males from the weaker, shorter signals of females.

A professed Darwinist would say that this ability evolved because the fish did not see well in the muddy water and the current-generating ability, which just emerged by chance, was necessary for survival. But what is needed for the functioning of such a multi-purpose electric system? First, is the current-generating organs, which are quite complicated. Second, the fish must be able to pick up electrically generated signals, for which purpose it needs a special organ on several points of the body. Ichthyologists furthermore pointed out that the brain of current-generating fish (the stimulus-processing field and the VIIth cranial nerve) differs from that of other fish. Without these special traits, electric eels would not be able to interpret incoming signals. And there is one more triviality: the fish is protected against the adverse effects of the current generated by itself by a thick layer of fat, which also covers muscles and nerves.

These organs all have to be present simultaneously in order for the electric eel to be able to generate electricity and to pick up and interpret signals coming to it. The system does not function if only parts of it are present. If, for example, only the insulating fatty layer had been missing, but by some miracle, all the other organs would have appeared all at once, the inventive explorer—the first fish to have this ability—would have electrocuted itself at the outset of its short evolutionary career with the first tentative electric shock.

In a chapter of *The Origin of Species* titled "Difficulties of the Theory," Charles Darwin himself was perplexed by the origin of species with electric organs. He revealed his helplessness with engaging honesty: "The electric organs of fishes offer another case of special difficulty; it is impossible to conceive by what steps these wondrous organs have been produced." It is more likely that living beings able to communicate with electric signals did not evolve over millions of years but are the design of a perfect electrical engineer.

The electric ray produces electricity. A system suitable for this supposes the simultaneous presence of numerous factors.

Tone setters

Acoustic communication is one of the most widespread ways of exchanging information in the animal world. Two advantages of sound are that it spreads quickly in all directions from the sound generator and that it is possible to transmit great amounts of information with it. Acoustic signals of different animal groups assume various functions. They can play a role in the communication between competing members of the same species in the form of menacing or defensive acoustic signals. They can also signal the approach of predators and alarm other members of the group. Sound emission plays an essential role in communication between members of animal communities. Social species may emit specific sounds for calling, gathering, greeting, begging, courting, or indicating fright, danger, or food. Some kind of "speech" often bonds the relationship between the young and their parents.

First we will examine the acoustic signals of insects. The male cricket, for example, sings three different kinds of tunes: one for giving information of his whereabouts, one for courting, and one for discouraging competitors. Crickets produce these sounds by rubbing special surfaces together at the stem of their wings. On the lower side of one of the wings, there are small protuberances that are like the teeth of a comb. The plectrum of the harp is a row of hard pegs on the edge of the other wing of the troubadour.

Besides the sound-emitting organ, naturally an appropriate sound-perception organ is also needed. The organ of hearing of crickets and katydids is in their tibia! There are two slits on

Cicadas are famous for their loud music.

68

Katydids hear with the help of a tiny organ on their leg.

the tibia of their forelegs. The sound enters the organ of hearing through these slits, where the eardrum reacts to incoming sounds by displacement. The displacement of the membrane stimulates the adequate sensor cells, which are surrounded by protective scopulate cells and attachment cells. All the parts of this perfectly functioning minute apparatus have to be in the appropriate place for perception to take place. The slits, the tympanic cavity separated by the membrane, the sensor cells, and the neurons going to the nerve center—all are necessary components of this sound system. (This is obviously a simplified description of a highly complicated system.)

What can be the origin of the hearing mechanism of crickets? For effective communication, both the plucked-sound-emitting organ and the complex hearing organ are necessary. And of course, we should not forget that insects also have to be able to understand the different signals of each other. Explain all this based on the fundamental assumption of the theory of evolution: namely, that a series of small, consecutive changes (all beneficial to the ancestors of crickets) occurred in a way to provide a benefit for survival against their competitors. This kind of explanation is impossible, simply because one should convincingly demonstrate that these three

The cricket "plays the violin" with its wing. Could nature be able to create such a sophisticated and precise instrument by mere chance?

phenomena (the instrument, the ear, and the code system) evolved simultaneously. It is also interesting that this organ, which works on the rubbing principle, is located in different places in different insects. Certain crickets rub their mandibles together, others produce a clapping sound with a row of pegs on their tibia, still others rub the raised stridulatory veins of their wings. The sound formation of species of true bugs (*Heteroptera*) is similarly varied. These species are allegedly related through their evolution, but remarkable differences in the position and mechanism of their organs of sound formation make it improbable that there is any genealogical relationship between them.

Growling, croaking and grunting fish

Ichthyologists used to think fish were mute, but it turns out that quite a few, especially among those species living in the Pacific Ocean and the northeastern Atlantic Ocean, are able to emit sounds. Reported sound signals among fish include rustling, humming, growling, croaking, and grunting, to mention a few. We do not know the information content of all sounds (or if they are all meaningful), but we do know that fish use different sounds to call each other, signal danger, share food searching information, and express their amorous mood. Most of them use one or two, but the more verbose ones may choose from five different sounds.

Some of the "loudmouthed" fish produce a sound by rubbing two elements of their bony skeleton together. For example, grunts (*Haemulon sp.*), surgeonfish (*Acanthurus sp.*), and trevallies (*Caranx sp.*) grind their pharyngeal teeth. Others make a noise by rubbing their teeth on their jaw, on their fins, or on some other mobile piece of bone. The growling sound of the ocean sunfish (*Mola mola*) comes from its bony jaw plate.

In another group of "talking fish," the swim bladder helps in generating sound. The primary purpose of the swim bladder, filled with gas, is to ensure the buoyancy of the fish. By rhythmical contraction of the trunk muscles, or some other special muscles, the fish causes it to vibrate. The muscles contract the front part of the bladder up to 100 times per second. The sounds thus produced resemble drumbeats, or sometimes growling, snarling, humming, and even grunting. If millions of Atlantic croakers (*Micropogon undulatus*) gather in a bay, they are able to make even a 110-decibel noise this way.

Similarly interesting is the method by which bony fish perceive sound waves. The sounds spreading in the water go through their bodies and make their swim bladder vibrate. The surface of the swim bladder is read by

70

auditory ossicles (like the needle of a phonograph reads a record), which then transmit the vibrations onto ear stones of different sizes, resembling organ pipes.

As with insects, the hearing and sound-producing processes of fish raise doubts about evolutionary theory. It is true that certain sound-emitting organs (teeth, fins, jaws, and the swim bladder) also assume functions other than their basic function in the body of the animal, but there is no answer to the question

muscles vibrating the swim bladder. It is not possible that such muscles, which assume separate functions and are able to contract very rapidly, developed gradually. On the other hand, their sudden emergence, by a single genetic mutation, is inconceivable, precisely because this would have necessitated the sudden and concerted change of hundreds of details in the genetic code of the animal, the probability of which is infinitesimal.

In the submarine hodge-podge of sounds, every species understands those signals meant for them. The details of how these species-specific communication systems developed are also unexplained. These signal systems require a unified decoding within a given community; in other words, the signs (in this case, the sound signals) have to imply a specific meaning that is the same for all members. But when did members of different fish species carry on conciliatory discussions in order to be able to understand messages of fellow members of the same species?

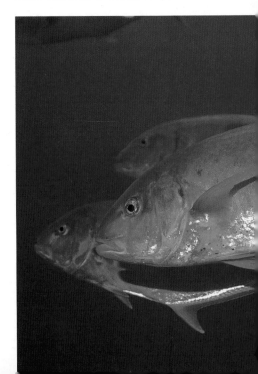

Surgeonfish and mackerels create sounds by rubbing their pharyngeal teeth together.

of exactly what made the first fish use these parts of its body for some other task. Even if this fish had carried out some "language reform," its fellows (not having taken advantage of such abilities) would not have understood its intention at all. Thus the unappreciated revolutionary would have gotten zero benefit from the commotion.

Besides this, there are unique elements in the sound formation of fish, such as the special

The origin of the sound-emitting and sound-perceiving organs and code system of insects cannot be explained by gradual evolution.

Notes—or improvisation?

We could say much more about the wonderful world of the sounds of birds and mammals, especially, for example, whales. We could wonder at the extraordinary sound-generating organs of the animals and for what purposes they use their different acoustic signals. However, the list of examples would be infinitely long. Therefore, we will instead focus on a few interesting but more general phenomena.

For example, in every case the frequency of emitted sounds is in harmony with the auditory capabilities of members of the same species. Katydids emit high-frequency sounds; their organ of hearing is also sensitive to these. Crickets produce chirring of a lower tone; their "ear" is also able to hear that. This same attunement is also demonstrable in birds. According to leading representatives of

evolutionism, this harmony is merely a product of the workings of nature's blind processes. But the "transmitters and receivers" of animals perfectly match their physical parameters, and the messages encoded in the sounds carry a unified meaning for all members of the given species. They know exactly what acoustic signals they have to emit under certain circumstances; at the same time, those receiving the signal understand the meaning of each sound. They are also fully aware of which sounds are meant for them and which ones are not. In a noisy forest, where a human ear hears only cacophony, each bird hears messages meant only for it.

In our view, the living world loudly testifies that a supernatural, intelligent engineer created perfectly matching organs to emit and receive sound. And the variegated code-systems enabling communication indicate that this designer is quite good at creating languages and informatics.

A counterargument may raise the point that not all these animals are born with a complete, predetermined communication sound system. Some of them also acquire signals serving different purposes during their lifetime (usually in the early period) from their parents and other

An inner program makes birds sing specific songs.

The chaffinch works with ready-made material: different songs serve different purposes, and the chaffinch even slightly modifies them in some cases. It has not only limits, but some freedom, too.

72

Visual signs on a
creature's body are clear
messages for whoever
sees them, independent
of their owner's
intentions.

members of the same species. Birds, for example, produce songs of characteristic form, structure, and quality. These programs are usually inherent, but individual experience and practice also play a part in their execution.

Chaffinches (*Fringilla coelebs*) are able to sing more than twenty stanzas. They court with three clearly distinctive songs in different stages of the mating cycle. They use at least three kinds of alarm cries: one when they are ready to fight, another when they are hurt, and the third when in a provocative mood. The loud, boisterous song of the chaffinch begins slowly, then speeds up, and finally ends in an ornamental motif. But the song of each individual slightly differs from that of others, and one can even discover dialects according to territories. Moreover, among the stanzas sung by chaffinches there are three characteristic ones that individuals brought up without their parents, in isolation, cannot sing. Young chaffinches can learn this sound sample only by imitating other members of their

species. In other words, they do not receive everything instinctually but complement their repertoire by learning.

Nevertheless, this "open program" does not at all contradict the assumption that there is an original composer in the background of all these animal sounds. There are improvisatory musical styles where the author only specifies the instrument, a certain register, and a few motifs, and then the performer presents its unique, although in some respects fixed, performance within these limits. Similarly, there are precisely definable sound types in the tonal system of the different animal species. Reptiles, for example, are able to produce an average of four different sounds, while monkeys, depending on the species, can produce five to thirty-six sounds. Sounds usually have a well-defined meaning in every species. But in some cases, as with songbirds, there is room for variety. Males of the same species can sing somewhat different tunes. Individual differences also help the birds in differentiating between each other.

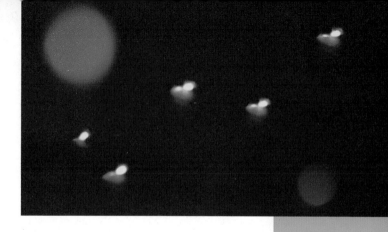

Consequently, it becomes understandable why different communities of the same species chirp in different dialects in geographically distant territories. Despite these dialects, characteristic ways of sound formation and tune types always remain the same. It is possible that the composer designed the basic characteristics of the songs of the species, but left room for individual variations inherited culturally by adoption.

The visible message

Colors, different light emissions, poses, and gestures transmit visible signals in the animal kingdom. Visual marks on the exterior body have several advantages, such as their striking and lasting effects. One drawback, however, is that they are usually not visible at night. Recognition of colors and marks is also hampered by natural features (e.g., dense vegetation), and is not as good for long-distance communication as sound is. Despite this, members of the animal kingdom transmit information in this way, both within a single species and between species. In the chapter "Defense, Disguise, Deception," we have presented a few examples of signs "painted" on skin, fur, or pigment that are meant to keep off or scare away predators.

Light signals

Optical marks "tattooed" on the body surface of animals passively relay one or more messages to the observer. Bearers of these patterns have only to be visible to convey the information—they don't have to *do* anything. Within some animal groups, however, there are light-emitting species that can actively telecommunicate self-produced rays. Light emission by oxidation, in the course of metabolic processes, is called bioluminescence.

Lantern-eye fish communicate with a natural light organ. They emit light from liquid-filled glands under their eyes. The glands contain millions of bacteria, which as a side

effect of the fish's vital processes, are bioluminescent. The light helps scare off predators or intruding members of the same species and illuminates prey, or the way. These fish can hide or cover their light organ, making it possible to transmit messages by way of flashes. The splitfin flashlightfish (*Anomalops katoptron*) can "switch off" its light by turning its light organ inward. The eyelight fish (*Photoblepharon palpebratus*) does the same by letting down an eyelid-like skin fold. Such abilities are obviously quite useful at depths where light is dim or nonexistent. But this does not explain the source of the necessary anatomical accessories—the gland suitable to store the bacteria, the "blind" allowing the obscuration and innervation of the organ, the light-emitting protozoa, etc. The theory of gradual evolution does not convincingly explain these phenomena because for such functions to take place all the necessary parts have to be working together, simultaneously. They are useless separate from each other or in half-developed stages.

Body language

Animals can also express their mood toward or relationship to another animal by various postures. Wolves, jackals, and hyenas, living and hunting in packs, express their sentiments, position within the pack, or amicable or aggressive intentions by a system of pose signals. In wolves, researchers distinguished fourteen tail poses, eight head poses, eight ear poses, and six body poses—each having

74

different meanings. Using these poses, wolves are able to convey a variety of messages to members of their species: indifference, confidence, uncertainty, friendly submission, subordination, threat, aggressive intentions, and more. It is quite interesting, for example, that when a wolf defeated by its pack-mate gives in by lying on its back, it offers the most vulnerable point—its throat—to the victor. The winner of the fight instinctively refrains from killing or seriously injuring the defeated one. It reacts to the surrender by ending the fight.

This behavior, observable in contests of dominance, is thought provoking. How could this habit of the defeated animals, offering the most vital point of the body to their adversary, have developed? How could they have known that their defeater will react to their submission with mercy and not with a "mercy bite"? And how could the winners' habit of not harming their totally defeated adversary have developed? It is undoubtedly beneficial for the species if members do not kill each other in fights for power. But it is very unlikely that a predator absorbed in a fight would rationally think about the matter. It is much easier to conceive that pack-mate-sparing inhibitions are a provision given by a merciful, instinct-creating intelligence.

In the gestural language of wolves, everything has a meaning: the position of the tail, the head, the ears, and the whole body. Wolves understand each other quite well.

Probably they disagree, too. Representatives of anti-evolutionist views rarely get the opportunity to speak at forums that promote science.

The language of dance

Different motions and series of movements can also have meaning in the animal world. Motion serves to scare off attackers, express aggression and intentions of attack, or indicate the exact location of food.

Honeybees (*Apis mellifera*), for example, use motion to convey food location. When a worker bee comes back to the beehive from a bountiful flower field, it performs a special dance. This dance informs other workers waiting in the beehive which direction and how far they should fly for the food. The form of the typical dance resembles the shape of a compressed, horizontal "8." The dancer runs in a straight line to form the center of the eight, meanwhile vigorously swaying its body to the right and left to form the circles. The other bees gather around it and watch the performance. The bee performs its dance in the beehive on a vertical honeycomb. In the straight section of the mobilizing dance, the little bee moves upward if the food source is in the sun's direction. If the food source is thirty degrees to the left from the horizontal direction of the sun, the straight part of the bee's dance will also deviate from the vertical by thirty degrees to the left. In other words, it is able to transform horizontal directions to a vertical surface! The number of times the bee sways its abdomen indicates the distance of the food. An average sway corresponds to about 225 feet if the food is near the beehive. This abstract language is quite an impressive accomplishment for a little insect that is less than an inch in length. The language of dance contains mutually intelligible conventions, as if the bees were all using a well worked-out, fixed code system in their exchange of information.

Bees use the language of dance in the course of swarming as well. The colony multiplies by scissiparity—in spring, half the beehive splits off and seeks a new home. Scouts look for an appropriate place for the nest hole and communicate the characteristics of possible places through dance. For example, its size (the ideal airspace is 10.5 quarts), its distance from the original bee family (it should be neither too far nor too close), its altitude above ground level (best is around 9 yards), the direction of its entrance, and whether it is drafty or full of chinks. After two to three days of negotiations, scouts democratically arrive at an agreement, and the swarm sets off to its new dwelling. This amazes researchers, but

The messenger bee informs the others about the direction and distance of food with a complex dance.

Bees are able to project horizontal directions onto the vertical plane of the honeycomb.

76

The abstract method of expression of the tiny bees is an object of wonder for scientists.

they still cannot explain how natural selection could have programmed such highly complex behavior into these small brains. It is highly improbable that the womb of Mother Nature would have given birth to such creatures without any external direction.

Austrian ethologist Karl von Frisch won the Nobel Prize in 1973 for having mapped the informative dance of bees. However, we may wonder for whom we should have the greatest regard—for the bees performing such a complex communications system, for researcher von Frisch who discovered this, or for the choreographer who created this entire language of dance?

Born with a dictionary

In this chapter we have discussed major types of information exchange between animals. Among these, we have presented cases to explain the way that animals communicate, as characterized from birth. They instinctively apply communication codes correctly. Some codes carry an automatic message to other animals, and some are congenital, based on scents, sounds or visual signs. Their origin is more than mystical, and modern science can support its guesses relating to them neither theoretically nor experimentally. The examples in this chapter seem to indicate that

Whom does it salute? The discoverer of its dance language, or its designer?

animals are born with picture-, sound-, and scent-dictionaries that are characteristic of their own species from time immemorial. Substantiating this is the fact that the existence and functioning of sign languages presupposes the mutual knowledge of signals from both "speakers" and "recipients." It is impossible that such sign systems evolved gradually, since the inventor of a new sign could not have let other members of the same species know what it meant by the new

If the new feeding place is situated seventy degrees away from the sun, the axis of the messenger bee's dance will deviate seventy degrees from the vertical.

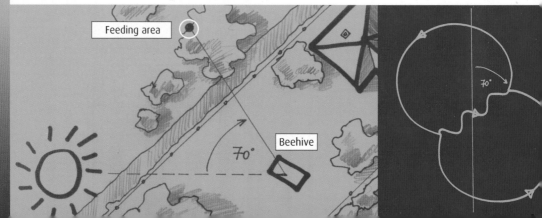

Feeding area

Beehive

70°

70°

Vervet monkeys have to learn how to use different sound signals properly. But even the origin of the learning ability is itself obscure.

signal. In other words, new communication signals would have fallen on deaf ears. All members have to use and understand the specific signs simultaneously. We again face a phenomenon that the theory of gradual evolution cannot explain. It is impossible to conceive of the multitude of animal codes without the existence of a preliminary plan, without a language-creating intelligence that first created the signs and the meanings matching them. Any code system has a meaning if, and only if, members of the communicating community use and understand the signs of the system simultaneously and uniformly.

It is true, however, that some animal "languages" have certain elements that are not entirely congenital; they are partly acquired by learning. Vervet monkeys (*Cercopithecus sp.*), for example, emit different sounds in the presence of different predators. They announce leopards, snakes, and eagles in a different way (they even have separate alarm signals for flying and landing eagles). Young vervet monkeys have to learn how to use and interpret different sound signals in the appropriate way. The origin of this learning ability, however, is no less obscure than that of linguistic elements received ready-made. It seems that living beings have come into existence according to a plan that had already determined that part of their communication tools must innately be ready to use, and others must be learned in the course of their development.

The vocabulary of different groups of animals and species is limited (as are their anatomical and learning abilities). The relative stability of these limits indicate that the ability to learn, and to what degree, may very likely come from a higher, systematically functioning intelligence.

We do not mean to say that animals are like robots, reacting to external stimuli only mechanically, according to the instructions "programmed" into them. In fact, we are convinced that each living thing is a unique individual and, within the limits of its species, has a unique personality. But abilities and instincts have predetermined limits for each species.

Man is totally different

Among researchers of animal communication, there is unanimous agreement that the "language" of animals greatly differs from any of the human languages. The vocabulary of animals, which rarely consists of more than a dozen units, is very modest compared to human speech. The lexicon of any European language numbers at least 100,000 words. The difference is even more striking if we consider that the sounds and signals of animals are merely indicators of needs or position. Humans, however, can combine words in an infinite number of ways. We use abstract notions and complex syntactical units; we express subtle thoughts. Thus messages of animals are not like human language; they are not able to transmit exact conceptual notions, composed according to the intention of the speaker. Other than humanity, no species of living being is known to have such abilities. In animal sign language, the means of communication are mostly innate; they are

Left turn! Each living being is a separate individual, and within the limits of its species, has a unique personality.

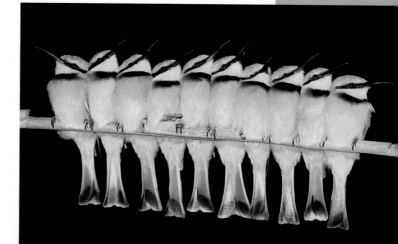

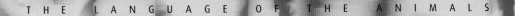

limited to visual, acoustic, chemical, elect-rical, and touch signs and involve only stimuli and responses.

Our conclusion is that animal languages were created by an intelligent designer as lesser or greater "traveler's dictionaries" for different living beings. These systems of signs, however, are markedly different from human language; the ability of animal to commu-nicate is generally limited and much narrower than that of humans.

One may ask with good reason: What was the purpose of the supposed designer in creating animal communication systems? What is the use of all this designing? Why do humans (as opposed to animals) have the ability of abstract thought and complex speech? We will address these questions in the last chapter.

78

Fly-by-night
wanderers or expert navigators?

Fly-by-Night Wanderers or Expert Navigators?

The periodic and regular displacement of groups of living beings belonging to the same species is called migration. Animals that migrate in one-year cycles—insects, crabs, fish, birds, mammals—often know surprisingly well when to leave and in which direction to travel. Their ability to orientate is amazing.

80

Sea turtles cover thousands of miles during their strange wanderings.

Animals have an inner sense of direction by which they are able to perceive and process the three directions of space (up and down, forward and backward, left and right). Yet this alone is not enough for their successful migration. They also need the ability to determine their exact location and the direction to travel, which they achieve with the help of reference points in the environment, such as hills, rivers, or other objects.

For migrants, the sense of direction is essential, but it is also indispensable for any animal to be able to move quickly and effectively within its environment. Among non-migrants (bees and ants, for example), there are a number of species in which this ability is highly developed. In the following pages, we will explore some extraordinary examples of this mystery.

When the time comes, members of many crab species set off on a journey to mate. The origin of the inner clock of living beings is quite mysterious.

Ant map

Desert ants (*Cataglyphis bicolor*) are true champions of orientation. Unlike other insects, they prowl in the Sahara even in the noonday hours, although the soil surface becomes as hot as 70° C (158° F). Exposure to such temperatures for a certain amount of time would mean certain death for insects or other small animals. Desert ants therefore build their nest underground and come to the surface to get food only periodically, ten to fifteen times a day.

Leaving the nest, an ant roves over a 200-square yard area, zigzagging on hot sand, searching for food (mostly dead insects). The moment it finds food, it returns straight to its underground dwelling by the shortest way. Other ant species follow their own scent trails and go back the same way they came. But desert ants can tell exactly the shortest way back to the nest, regardless of how many zigzags, turns, and curves they made along the way. Have you ever been in an unfamiliar city, and after having made four or five turns, tried to get back to where you started? If so, you can understand what a remarkable feat the desert ant performs, especially since it is unaided by landmarks and can see only sand everywhere. How is it able to find the right direction?

Nowadays, satellites and computers facilitate urban traffic. A satellite registers the location of the car and transmits the coordinates to the computer built in the car. The driver specifies the destination, and the shortest way there immediately appears on the screen. In the tiny ant brain, much smaller than a cubic millimeter, a function just as complex takes place. How? The blazing sun assists the ant. With its compound eye, the ant is able to discern polarized light (in which sunrays oscillate in the same plane at angles depending on the sun's position). While searching for food, the ant stops at regular intervals, turns its head right and left, and examines the polarized light map of the sky. From this, it determines the way home.

Every desert ant is able to accomplish this feat. What is the origin of this ability? Could orientation based on polarized light have evolved gradually, over thousands of years? Evolutionists may argue that desert ants could have evolved from another, non-desert-dwelling ant species that still orientated in the traditional way—in the beginning it left scent trails and "switched" only gradually to orienting by light and living in the desert. But such an idea should be supported with an explanation of how the ability to perceive polarized light and to analyze direction appeared in ants. This

82

knowledge is far too complex to be the product of an accidental genetic mutation. The insect is either capable of this behavior, including all the tiny details, or it isn't. If this ability developed "in the course of long millennia," each desert ant would have died during its first expedition for food—just as happens occasionally now to ants that make a miscalculation and get lost. If only "errant" ants had existed in the past, the second generation would not have been born.

Salmon: back to the sender

Salmon (*Oncorhynchus sp.*) are born in fresh water rivers and springs, but they do not develop there fully. Full-grown individuals live in the sea, but before the mating season, they leave the salty water because their eggs can hatch only in crystal-clear fresh water, which is rich in oxygen. For spawning, salmon return to the shallow waters of upper reaches of rivers (for example, in a clear mountain creek) and lay their eggs there. There are many salmon species. One major group lives in the Atlantic Ocean, another in the Pacific. From among the latter, we will examine the sockeye salmon (*Oncorhynchus nerka*).

Young salmon of this species hatch near the headwaters of North American rivers. Later they follow the river's current to the ocean. In the sea, they are predators, hunting for smaller fish in large areas. Their shoals can venture up to 350 miles from the shore. Until they are six years old, they live in the ocean as if they had totally forgotten their birthplace.

After six years, in early summer, they all return to the mouth of the same river from which they entered the sea. After gathering for three to four days, their seemingly infinite

procession sets off against the river's current, back to the upper parts of the river. Nothing can stop them! With unbelievable energy, they struggle through yard-high sand banks, rocks, and stranded tree trunks in shallower reaches. They fight their way through rapids, and they do not shirk from falls. With powerful strokes of their caudal fins, they can spring a yard high, again and again, until they can continue on their way.

At branches of rivers or streams, they choose with unfailing certainty the direction leading to the place they were born six years earlier. From among the countless branches, they always choose the one they swam down when they were little fish. How do they know the right way? According to experiments, salmon orient by the help of their sense of smell and taste (in their case, it is hard to separate the two). They navigate by the "smell" of the water, which is quite surprising because there is hardly any detectable chemical difference among these crystal-clear mountain waters. When they were young, they recorded the scent of waters they passed through on their journey to the sea, and these memories remain even after living six years in salt water! Using this uncanny ability, they swim upstream as far as 1,200 miles.

Along the way, both males and females undergo considerable anatomical changes that facilitate their reproduction. Their internal organs contract, and their sexual organs grow larger. By the time they reach their spawning place, females are almost bursting with eggs. At the end, they arrive at exactly the same rivulet in which they were born years before; now it is their turn to start a new generation. After mating, males hollow out a shallow little basin in the gravel in which the females lay their

thousands of eggs. After fertilizing the eggs, most of the sockeye salmon die from complete exhaustion. But their offspring will be back in six years, and the species will continue.

Secrets under the water

The behavior of salmon seems quite synchronous. According to the evolutionist view, their ancestors were similar to trout, living exclusively in rivers. But there is no evidence afloat of how such freshwater fish could have acquired the traits of the sockeye salmon. Despite rambling several thousand miles in the ocean, they unfailingly find the mouth of the river from which they came. They struggle back—even over a thousand miles—to their place of birth, via exactly the same route they took to the ocean by recalling the smells of the route in reverse order. Their body undergoes a transformation necessary

for reproduction precisely at that time, and after having reached their destination, they mate and die. This occurrence is far too complex to have happened by chance transformations.

A first-class mystery

Navigation is the art of reaching a destination. To be successful, an animal not only has to know exactly which direction it should go, but also where its starting point is. They are able to find and stick to the right direction by recording, processing, and correctly applying different kinds of information. Birds use at least three independent "compasses" for navigation: the sun compass, the star map, and earth's magnetism.

In daytime, birds use the sun as a compass. The sun's position changes by the minute, and they adjust their orientation accordingly. If clouds obscure the sun, birds

Salmon struggle to return to their birthplace via the same route they once left it. After six years they still remember scents of their route.

In early summer, sockeye salmon gather at the mouth of the river where they were born. No one knows how they learn of the gathering.

use the patterns of the polarized light, invisible to the human eye, to locate the planet's relative position.

Birds migrating at night determine their position from the constellations. This is quite an impressive achievement, especially if we consider that the starry sky looks different depending on longitude and season. Besides, starlight is not as bright as sunlight; therefore, birds have to scrutinize the sky to identify constellations.

The magnetic field of the earth is a series of lines of force that form certain angles relative to the earth's surface. At the poles, the lines are almost perpendicular to the earth, while at the equator they are parallel to it. Birds are able to determine their location by the angle enclosed by the earth and the magnetic lines of force.

Many other important factors play a part in the success of navigation. Among them are memorizing the features of the terrain (e.g., islands, bays, coastlines), perception of smells and sounds (and infra-sounds), changes of atmospheric pressure, and even differences in gravitational force. However, we know very little about exactly how birds orientate and how they process information in the course of

These birds can always find their way back to their loft.

their migration (to what extent they rely on which types of orientation, how they connect them, etc.). What little we do know is already astonishing!

The reliable postman

Certain animals have exceptional navigational faculties. Domesticated rock doves (*Columba livia domestica*), for example, are admired for this ability. It is a mystery how they can orientate so excellently. They can find their way back to their loft from almost anywhere (from any direction, even from great distances) even if they were transported from there in a closed box.

Many experiments have examined the orientation of domesticated rock doves, but the results obtained are still equivocal. Some researchers assume that doves use a map-and-compass strategy. The birds use the sun as a compass, and by the help of their inner clock, compensate for the sun's motion. This means that if the dove is watching the sun at 10 a.m. from a place with the latitude of 45° north and the longitude of 19° east, then it can calculate with the precision of a sextant which direction and at what speed the sun will move. According to some scientists, doves (and other animals using the sun compass) learn all this by observing the sun's movement several times while they are young. Even if these assumptions are correct, it is still amazing that birds are born with the ability to acquire and apply this complex knowledge.

Moreover, rock doves found their way home even in experiments in which their sight was hampered by opaque contact lenses; they could not determine their position by the sun or the landmarks of their route. Several theories exist concerning other mechanisms in the orientation of doves, but their exact method of navigating home is still not resolved. Their absolute ability of location and orientation is especially unusual. Domesticated rock doves (and some other bird species) can assess where they are even if they did not see how they got there—and they return home by

85

The ancestor of the domesticated rock dove (also known as the "homing pigeon"): the rock dove.

White storks (below), even if carried in a closed box, have the ability to fly in the right direction after a short evaluation of their position.

Where does their extraordinary orientation ability come from?

the shortest possible way. A Polish researcher named Wodiczky took adult white storks out of their nests and transported them to Israel. When he let them free, the storks calmly did a few circles in the air and then headed in the direction of their nest in a beeline. The quickest of them made the 1,410 kilometer-long distance in 196 hours. This is as if someone blindfolded and carried us several thousand kilometers away. Then, at the unknown place, this person took the blindfold off, and we immediately determined the right direction and proceeded home by the shortest route possible.

It is obvious that in addition to their sight, birds rely on other special senses in the course of their migration and orientation. Domesticated rock doves, for example, have exceptional faculties of perception. They perceive ultraviolet and polarized light, they are very sensitive to surface vibrations, and are able to hear even 0.1 Hz frequency. The main question is not which of these they rely on most in navigation, but where their extraordinary sense of direction comes from. Should we really believe that this whole system of perceiving and harmonizing directions is a result of an unexplainable series of genetic accidents?

Let us imagine that we have to create an airplane that is able to register the positions of the sun and the stars, and based on these, locate its position while it also takes into account the daily and yearly movement of the planets. Besides this, the aircraft should also be able to register and process smells and sounds of the environment, changes in the earth's magnetism, as well as ultraviolet and polarized light, and by the help of any of these, determine the right direction. And finally, it should recognize when it reaches its destination. If we wanted to transform all this from blueprint into fact, we would need complicated sensor apparatuses requiring significant space, as well as high-performance computers. The most sophisticated airplanes of today cannot function to this capacity. Despite that, these airplanes have a huge instrument panel with many complicated instruments. On the other hand, the "avionics" of birds is miniaturized, extremely reliable, and its maintenance is cost-free.

A stop en route. Doves, by their mysterious instincts, solve the complicated navigational tasks with natural simplicity.

To successfully navigate and drive a space shuttle to its destination, the concerted cooperation of many people and instruments is required. For grey herons (pictured page opposite, top) it is not a great problem at all.

And birds do not need a long time to train, like human pilots. The "bird-brained" birds easily execute these extraordinary navigational tasks. If developing the precision instruments of an airplane requires many plans and a highly developed intelligence, how could a substantially more complex "apparatus" have developed by itself?

Wanderers of the sky

The most amazing wanderers of the animal kingdom are migratory birds. The fascinating capabilities of migratory birds greatly increase the number of mysteries connected to orientation by animals.

Half of the world's bird species migrate annually and months later return to their nesting site. Birds migrate before winter to a warmer climate that provides adequate food. Migration routes are quite different depending on the species. It would require a voluminous atlas to depict detailed maps of their routes. The distances covered also vary. There are three categories pertaining to distance: short-, medium-, and long-distance migrants. Some winged wanderers of the sky travel several thousands—even tens of thousands—of miles. Let's examine some of these globetrotting wonders.

White-winged black terns. Wanderers of the sky often cover several thousand miles during their migrations, arriving at their destination infallibly.

The bird of the brightness

The arctic tern (*Sterna paradiseae*) is the record holder for distance among migratory animals. This gull species, with a body weight of 3–4 ounces and a wingspan of 29–33 inches, flies no less than 22,000 miles every year during its marathon from the Arctic to the Antarctic and back. This is comparable to flying around the world every year.

Its nesting area is in the northernmost dry lands of the northern hemisphere—Greenland and the polar regions of Canada and Siberia, and sometimes even beyond the Arctic Circle. Its wintering area, on the other hand, is at the southernmost part of the globe at the edges of the Antarctic ice fields.

Arctic terns hatch their nestlings in the Arctic, from May until November. If an arctic tern pair finds a safe nesting place, abundant in food sources, they will return there every year. They migrate southward at the end of the reproductive period (ranging from about August until December). By the end of the southern summer, all arctic terns set off to escape the cold, dark winter months. Terns hatching in the polar regions of East Canada and Greenland leave their nesting sites and cross the Atlantic Ocean with the aid of the west winds to join the flocks of their European fellows hurrying southward. They fly south by the western coasts of Europe and Africa. A small percentage of them stay in South Africa, and the others, passing by the Cape of Good Hope, fly on to the islands around the Antarctic. The trip takes them ninety days.

During their stay at their southern "wintering area," it is also summer. Then in February, mature individuals (terns usually become mature at the age of three) again set off and do the entire journey in the opposite direction. They reach their northern nesting sites by May or June. Younger terns do not return to the Arctic in their first year but go around the Antarctic Circle counter-clockwise and spend the summer on the shores of the Pacific Ocean where there is plenty of food. In their third spring, they join the adults on their journey to the far-away nesting sites in the north.

The distance, in a straight line, between the nesting and wintering areas of terns is at least 9,400 miles. They could find plenty of areas suitable for wintering, which would provide their essential conditions of life, much closer than this; they do not need to undertake the risky crossing of the Atlantic Ocean. Then why do they choose the earth's two farthest regions as the locales for their life? What urges them to fly so far so often? Obviously, it is instinct. However, this does not answer the question. Where does this instinct, which

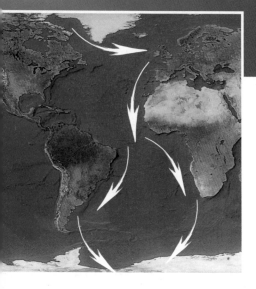

in New Zealand travel, for example, a distance of 3,750 miles to Middle and South Polynesia, though they could winter much closer if they chose Australia.

Some ornithologists try to make migration routes, which often seem somewhat illogical, more understandable by reasons relating to the history of the earth, the movements of continents, or the ice age. But because of the great variety of routes, these are often unsatisfactory explanations, as in the case of the arctic tern. Neither in the past nor present do we see such compelling circumstances that could have made this migration of extreme distances evolve gradually. And the idea that a genetic mutation suddenly motivated them to—presto!—move 9,400 kilometers away at the appropriate time and then move back a few months later, is utterly inconceivable.

Arctic terns spend most of their life in daylight, since the sun does not set beyond the Arctic Circle while they are there; the same

Sunlight-seeking birds fly almost incessantly by their migration instinct.

impels them to take long journeys and guides them to the right place, come from?

In the case of other birds, the question remains the same: Why do they migrate to a specific place at a specific time? It is almost inconceivable why they choose such distant wintering sites, while they often fly over lands providing suitable living conditions. The long-tailed koel (*Urodynamys taitensis*) and the golden-bronze cuckoo (*Chalcites lucidus*) living

Like other birds, this semi-palmated plover was banded in order to gather information on migration.

holds true for the Antarctic regions. They bathe in more sunlight in the course of one year than any other bird, or for that matter, any other creature on earth. Perhaps the arctic tern migrates only to be able to live constantly in daylight. Whatever the purpose, these travels should serve to enlighten us—the routes of birds were not created by a series of chance events; winged pilots of the sky got their training at a higher level.

the final destination without landing even once. This obviously requires extraordinary amounts of energy. Many factors influence the efficiency of the flight. The distance they can cover depends on the quantity of energy stored and the rate they use it.

The ruby-throated hummingbird (*Archilochus colubris*) weighs only about 0.1 ounce! This is the only colibri species nesting in the eastern part of North America. It spends the winter in Mexico and Central America. To do this, it crosses the Gulf of Mexico, a distance of almost 620 miles. At the end of the winter, it comes back. This is a tremendous challenge for a little 0.1-ounce bird, without food and rest. While crossing the Gulf, this bird flaps its wings seventy-five times per second for twenty-five hours without stopping. That is more than 6 million continuous wing strokes!

According to computer models based on metabolism studies, this feat is not possible for the hummingbird. There is simply not enough room in the little 0.1-ounce bird to store sufficient energy to make the journey; it should run out of fuel on the way. It is able to perform this feat by storing surplus fat in its body during the period before migration (it roughly doubles its weight) and by taking advantage of favorable tail winds. This sensational accomplishment raises a perplexing question: If the bird had evolved from a species that had not made the trip, how would it have known that it had to go on a fattening

The winged record holders, the arctic terns, cover more than 9,400 miles between their nesting area and wintering area. What prompts them to undertake this long journey?

Impossible journeys

One may contend that through long sections of the journey, terns fly by the coast, and being waterfowl, they can land on the waves if they get tired; this diminishes the significance of the flight record previously mentioned. However, many of them fly until they reach

Some migratory birds are able to rest on the ocean's waves. Others, however, cannot. Therefore, they can undertake longer journeys only after having stored a great amount of energy in their body.

The tiny ruby-throated hummingbird crosses the Gulf of Mexico using six million wing strokes. It prepares for the journey by going on an intensive fattening diet.

diet? If a species member tried to make the trip without the surplus fat, it would have failed. It is obvious that for this trip to be possible, someone had to preprogram the intelligence of the hummingbird.

Perfect strength management

The case of the American golden plover (*Pluvialis dominica*) is similar. This tiny bird flies from Alaska to Hawaii, covering more than 2,200 miles above the open ocean. Without any intake of energy (food) during the journey, how is the bird capable of flying this distance?

The reserve energy of birds is stored in the form of fat in their body. Shortly after their offspring learn to fly, the parents of the few-months-old golden plovers leave their young and "take a vacation"—they fly to Hawaii. They gain 2.5 ounces in a short time, adding more than half their existing body weight. This is their fuel reserve during the long journey. An average-sized golden plover weighs about seven ounces when it leaves Alaska, of which the above-mentioned 2.5 ounces is fat reserves. The weight of this winged champion cannot decrease to less than 4.5 ounces, because if all its reserves are exhausted, it will die.

Flying for one hour, the bird uses up 0.6 percent of its body weight. Thus it would need just under three ounces of fat to cover the 2,200 miles. In other words, by journey's end it would weigh only a little over 4.1

Hummingbirds, just like hawk moths, feed on the nectar of flowers.

ounces; after having flown for seventy-two hours, it would tumble into the ocean just under five hundred miles short of its destination. This rate of losing weight should be fatal.

How does the golden plover successfully reach the Hawaiian Islands? The economical choice of speed of the golden plover and the flying formation of the flock enable it to survive the impossible journey.

Every bird has an optimal flight speed. If it flies slower than that, it is difficult for it to stay up in the air, and if it flies faster, it uses extra energy to overcome atmospheric resistance. It is similar to when a car uses more gas above a certain speed. We can stop at a gas station to refuel, but the golden plover does not have this option. Along this ocean stretch, there is not one island, peninsula, or dry spot where it can land. And it cannot swim. The optimal, energy-saving flight speed varies among different bird species. It depends, among other things, on physical structure and plumage. In the case of the American golden plover, optimal speed is just a little under thirty-two miles per hour. The golden plover strictly adheres to this speed limit. But maintaining this rate only results in the bird not losing unnecessary energy.

How does it manage to decrease the energy need so its supply is sufficient and the bird does not plunge into the open sea? The flock saves energy by flying in a "V" formation. In the course of the flight, whirlwinds arise behind the birds' wings that help those behind them. The birds share the burden of the lead position in the formation by changing positions from time to time. Thus all the members of the flock can save as much as twenty-three percent of their energy during their flight by the help of whirlwinds. This is how it is possible for the golden plover to use only 2.24 ounces of fat from its reserves instead of the calculated 2.9 ounces. It reaches its destination with a few grams of contingency reserves, which it can draw upon in case of occasional headwinds. The absolute precision of the calculations of nature's engineer shames even aircraft engineers.

Could the migration of the golden plover have developed by evolution? Suppose that the first plovers-to-be species migrated only 600 miles, and then drowned. The next generation covered 750 miles, and then fell into the abyss. And the next generation got as far as 900 miles, and then the next... But if the first generation already drowned, how can we speak of any next generation—or any evolution?

Other unanswered questions also remain. Look at a map of the Pacific Ocean; the Hawaiian Islands are tiny specks in the middle of the ocean, surrounded on all sides by thousands of miles of sea. How do golden plovers even know these islands exist and exactly how far they are? Remember their surplus energy is just enough to make the trip; a slight distance miscalculation could be fatal. How do they know (or how would their ancestors have known) which direction to travel? Their navigational system is so precise they can hold or correct their course without any visible points of reference, even in cases when a storm drives them off course. Where does this ability come from? How do they know that a certain time before

setting out, they have to take more food to build up enough fat in their bodies? We can say that these are just the effects of instincts and hormones, but giving a scientific name to the wonder does not actually explain its origin.

Accessories of an expedition

Suppose we want to climb one of the peaks of the Himalayan Mountains. What will we need to do that? Certainly we should know exactly where we want to go and what route we will take to get there. We should make a

The American golden plover seems almost insignificant in its own environment. Its migrational achievement, however, is quite sensational. Although it does not know its destination, it flies an exact course to the Hawaiian Islands having stored the exact amount of energy needed for the trip.

94

It is not easy to get to the top. However, the migration of birds is an even more complex task.

timetable, calculating the time of departure and the phases and pace of the expedition until we reach the destination. We should have a map and a compass. We should make sure we take enough food and clothes of appropriate quality. We would also need ropes, pickaxes, hooks, carbines, and other items familiar to experienced mountaineers. We can see that organizing an expedition is a complex task. The migration of birds is not one bit simpler than this.

What do migratory birds need for a successful flight? Many animal species have a biological "clock" that accurately tells them what to do at a given time of their daily and yearly cycle. Bird species that cannot take nourishment during the flight begin to gain weight at the right time so they have sufficient energy for the flight. They set off at the right time, and they know when it is time to return.

The functioning of this inner clock is in itself a biological mystery. We know very little about how it works, and we know nothing about its origin. It is surely under hormonal regulation, but this is precisely what is surprising. It produces the exact hormones required at exactly the right time. It is true that the decrease of sunny hours in the fall can influence hormone functions, but this does not at all explain such a precise harmony between the biological changes taking place in birds and their requirements for successful migration.

We mentioned that we would need a considerable amount of food for our mountain expedition. Birds carry this as accumulated fat. It is interesting that each species accumulates exactly the amount of energy needed for the distance it travels. Some species put on only a few grams, but others increase their body weight as much as a

hundred percent before migration. With this supply they can fly 2,500 miles in five days.

To climb the Himalayas, we would need appropriate clothing and tools. It is also very important for wanderers of the sky to have a strong and durable feather-dress for their journey. Many birds prepare for the seasonal flight by "getting new clothes," a process called molting—shedding old feathers and replacing them with new ones.

The first flights of migratory birds also raise some doubts about evolutionary theory. They are in their original home, food is still abundant, and living conditions are appropriate. How do they know it's time to go? It's as if someone prompted them, or built in them the instruction that at this time of the year, they have to leave. It is also remarkable that "first-year students" of many species reach the destination of their flight alone, even if no one showed them the way. The cuckoo (*Cuculus canorus*), for instance, does not know its parents, since the cuckoo mother lays her egg in the nest of another bird and then leaves. In spite of this, young cuckoos still follow their parents' migration route—alone, without any acquired knowledge or external help!

In other bird species, in addition to the young having a sense of direction, the more experienced birds are capable of revising and correcting this inner direction if necessary. Trials made with starlings showed this. In Holland, researchers captured a flock that was ready for flight and released them in Switzerland. The young ones, since it was their first flight, flew in the "preprogrammed" southwestern direction and ended up in Spain. The older, experienced starlings could not be outsmarted. They started in the west-northwesterly direction, correcting the deviation, and went to their usual wintering areas in France, Great Britain, and Ireland. Thus the inner program of birds is not entirely blind and fixed. Due to their experience (and their previously mentioned "absolute ability of orientation," or range finding), they are able to make adjustments when necessary. It is quite interesting that young birds know the distance of the normal migration. If by some artificial intervention (such as artificial transportation), the route of young birds is shorter, they still cover the distance of the normal migration, passing beyond their original destination.

In the course of their flight, birds rely heavily on their navigational faculties, which are very complex, as described earlier. Even young birds with no migratory experience have the ability to tell the apparent center of rotation of stars and to adjust the direction of their flight to that. If we make a fake planetarium for them and rotate the sky in it, they will modify their projected course accordingly.

Migratory birds stick to their wintering areas; every year they return to the very same place unless external circumstances prevent them from doing so. It is feasible, therefore, that the direction and destination of their migration has been the same since time immemorial.

The information gained from studying the migration of birds also supports our opinion that a higher intelligence directs the behavior of living beings. We have listed only a portion of the anatomical and behavioral factors that birds require for the success of their migration. The above descriptions show that many complex abilities must be simultaneously present for migratory birds to perform such impressive feats, and these abilities and knowledge have to work in perfect harmony.

If we want to climb the highest peak of the Himalayas, Mount Everest, we have to create a detailed plan to be able to reach our goal. It would be foolish to think that merely by a series of fortunate accidents, in time we will suddenly find ourselves there. Not only do we have to make an all-encompassing plan, but we also have to execute every detail of it. If we disregard just a single factor (for example, we forget to take our shoes), our undertaking, despite all our efforts, could end in failure. The migratory system of birds, too, is able to function only in its entirety, and the superficial assumptions about its "gradual evolution" get caught in the filter of logical thinking.

Since when have birds migrated?

Scientists have given several reasons for the emergence of the migration of birds. Let's examine a few of them to see how tenable they are.

According to one of the assumptions concerning the migration of birds in Europe,

American little stints, like many other birds, migrate in flocks. This provides them with greater protection against predators. There are, however, individuals within the species that find their appropriate destination even alone, without any prior learning.

96

prior to the latest ice age, birds had been living only in the environs of present-day Southern Europe and the Sahara. At that time these areas received regular rainfall; therefore birds living there had plenty of food. Then, drought affected more and more areas, gradually deteriorating their living conditions and forcing them to go further north to hatch. From their nesting sites, they returned south in the winter, and then they commuted every year. As the desert extended further, the distance between the nesting and wintering areas grew bigger.

Paleontological evidence that shows that birds had also migrated in ages when the climate of the earth had been uniformly warm contradicts this theory. Fossils of birds show the wing index (the length of the first flight feather compared to the length of the whole wing) of birds of yore. The bigger this number is, the more probable it is that a species migrated. For example, the index is 16 for a wintering bird, 25–35 for a medium-

From among migrating starlings (orange) caught in the Netherlands and transported into Switzerland (white), the young ones followed the direction encoded in them after they were released, and so they landed in Spain (yellow). Older, more experienced individuals, however, realized that they had been "hijacked," and flew to their usual wintering place in northwest Europe (red).

distance migrant, and can be as much as 72 for a long-distance migrant. Fossils of birds of the distant past showed that certain species had wings typical of migratory birds even two

million years ago. In other words, birds migrated in the Tertiary period, too, when the climate would not have forced them to do so.

Another important consideration is that the migration of birds is not at all restricted to a north-south direction. Migration patterns vary. The redwing (*Turdus iliacus*), which hatches in Russia and Northern Europe, is an east-west migrator; it winters in Western and Southern Europe. Flamingos living in South Africa get to India with the help of the monsoon; they migrate from west to east and then return in January. And the albatross, after leaving nesting sites on the islands of the southern oceans, practically fly around the earth, parallel with the equator. Ice ages cannot be the cause of these migrations. In fact, the immense distances covered by many north-south migrants are actually not justified by the earlier extension of the ice sheet.

Other explanations for the cause of the migration of birds include the continental drift, changes in the temperature, the change in the length of daytime, nutrition problems, etc. But these assumptions are unable to provide a sensible explanation for the origin of migration, neither separately nor combined. Technical books admit that explanations of the origin of birds' ability to migrate are based heavily on assumptions. In other words, scientists do not have the foggiest idea where the complex migration patterns come from.

All explanations struggle with the same problems. The theory of evolution is based on the principle of gradualness and the premise that animal behavior is fixed in their genes. But the emergence of bird migration is often difficult to deduce even theoretically by assuming a step-by-step evolution. The golden plover finds the distant islands essential for its existence in the vast Pacific

Flying great egrets and two grey herons. The proportion of the length of the flight feathers and the total length of the wing tells us whether a bird is a migrant. The impression of the plumage of ancient birds reveals that they had been migrants, too.

97

Ocean with a sure touch. There can be no gradual development of this ability; it either knows where it has to go and is physically fit for the journey, or it does not know and is not fit to go. There can be no intermediate stages.

A popular idea is that long migration routes developed from shorter ones, and the shorter ones developed due to environmental factors or changes in the climate. It is true that even today there are birds that do not migrate, and there are also vagrants (e.g., pheasants) that stroll aimlessly to find places with more food and better climate. Besides these, there are short-distance, medium-distance, and long-distance migrants. Still, the conclusion that one type evolved from the other is totally unfounded. We have seen that migration does not simply mean the covering of a certain distance. It also supposes a complex anatomy and knowledge, and these factors differ greatly in birds of different migratory types. Thus the idea that these types have always existed parallel with each other is more acceptable. There have always been wintering birds (those that spend all seasons in the same place), vagrants, and winged wanderers migrating to short, medium, and long distances. It is very plausible that a higher intelligence determined the modes of migration characterizing the different species as well as shaped the physical structure, feeding, and mating habits of migratory birds.

Since when have birds migrated? They have migrated since time immemorial.

Points of controversy

Genetics also casts serious doubts on the theory of gradual evolution. Physical and intellectual traits connected to migration are "encoded" in thousands of links often separated from each other in the chains of DNA molecules comprising the genes of

South African flamingos migrate to India, and then return. Different bird species travel as if they were obeying the directions of a well-regulated aerial navigation.

98

birds. Since acquired knowledge does not appear in genes, how can we suppose that this complex genetic system governing migration evolved due to a series of wonderful chance events (mutations)? Instead of a "chain of accidents bordering on a miracle," it is more plausible that a superior consciousness created living beings and determined the characteristics of the migratory instinct of every single species.

The observation that groups of the same species living in different places migrate in different directions and to different places

also supports this conclusion. For example, blackcaps (*Sylvia atricapilla*) hatching in Western Europe migrate southwest, and those hatching in Eastern Europe migrate southeast. This may indicate that the higher intelligence coordinating the different systems of migration thinks not only in terms of species but also in terms of cohabiting communities of species (populations), and shapes their courses accordingly.

The migratory habits of birds is not nearly as precisely fixed as the timetable and routes of trains. It is true that the migration program of living beings is flexible (within certain limits). Birds, for example, are able to take account of the weather in assessing the most

favorable date, within a given period, for their departure. They do not set out for their journey as an alarm clock begins to ring at a set moment. This only shows that the inner instinct pushing them to migrate is not blind but adjustable to the circumstances. Although adjustments are possible, the birds cannot act completely independent of their migratory habits.

Sometimes it happens that some members of the same species migrate while others (those for whom the habitat is suitable even in wintertime) do not. This does not contradict the fact that in animals, there are inherently determined "programs" working. What we see is that the running of these programs depends on external circumstances, just as in computer science there are subroutines that run only if certain conditions are fulfilled. We can liken this to

Eastern white pelicans winter in North Africa, the Middle East, and the area around the Persian Gulf.

Pheasants wander around without any specific destination, just to find areas richer in food.

The Bohemian waxwing that nests in Canada, the United States, and the northern parts of Eurasia appears in cities during times of need.

the phenomenon occurring when in certain species only the young migrate while the older ones are stationary (these are called partially migratory species).

In summary, we can say that migration programs are not completely hard-and-fast. They are flexible to some extent depending on the circumstances. But their main features are fixed, and these are predetermined and cannot be changed. Acquired factors can also determine the details of migration, which the young acquire from the older ones, but basic elements of the mechanism of migration—when, where, and by which route they have to go, and when they have to return—are unchangeably part of the birds' intelligence. Perhaps they do not know exactly what the destination looks like, but they certainly know its direction and distance. This must have been the case in the past as well.

Birds of a feather...

Birds of a feather flock together, just as people of similar character become friends. As the Hungarian saying goes, one can recognize a bird by its feather and a man by his friends. And a solid scientific explanation is recognized by the fact that by a few basic assumptions, it is able to explain a multitude of phenomena.

There is a very simple explanation for the entire phenomenon of migrations. As the seasons change, weather conditions also change in many places, so much so that certain species cannot survive through seasonal changes. If the world with its variety of seasons was created by a cautious, judicious, highly intelligent being, then this creator made the earth a suitable dwelling for living beings in every season. Thus for the winter season, the creator equipped many living beings with an instinct that would direct them to a suitable dwelling. Animals obey this inner command when they set out on their migration, and this same inner direction makes them (by medium of hormones) return.

But if this is the case, why is it that caravans of the sky sometimes move seemingly unnecessary long distances? The answer is that in this way complex programs function in coordination. Routes and wintering areas of the species involved have been determined in such a way that they do not meet obstacles beyond their abilities—high mountains, long sea routes, or deserts impossible to fly across. Therefore, each species arrives at a temporary habitat suitable for it. Furthermore, this careful system of order circumvents the problem of species competing for the same habitat. This is

99

The inner clock of swallows indicates when it is time to gather and then to leave. In the same way, they "feel" when it is the right time to return. The source of this knowledge is a mystery.

The river kingfisher lives in Eurasia, North Africa and the Far East. Its northern populations migrate to the south to winter there.

100

how the "repartition of the world" is realized for the winter months, by which everyone gets to a safe place.

At first this explanation may seem a little naive and unusual because it presents our world as static, while it is obviously always changing. It is true that throughout the history of the earth certain bird species have changed or extended their habitats. However, their wintering areas have remained quite stable.

Only the evolutionary tales tell us "the destinations of migratory animals developed over millions of years." Observation does not support this view. However, there are several observations suggesting that migratory birds hereditarily adhere to, and have always adhered to, set routes and wintering areas. They seem to be obeying commands of aerial control from a higher order, which supplies each animal group with the appropriate inner urge (instincts) so each set out on their journey at the appropriate time. This control also ensures that each has the particular sense of time and navigational system to enable them to reach their destination.

Why should an intelligent world designer have created such an eventful living world? We will address this question in the last chapter.

Couples
and mating

Couples and Mating

In the previous chapters we dealt mostly with self-preservation activities of animals as individuals. Now we will focus on behavior in connection with the preservation of the entire race. First we will examine how individuals of opposite sexes find each other and what methods they use to entice their mates. Then we will examine a few species with extraordinary techniques of reproduction so astounding they inspire us to investigate the origins of systems of reproduction throughout the animal world.

102

Whale song

The anatomical structure of whales cannot have evolved from those of terrestrial animals by small genetic changes; their existence requires the simultaneous presence of their complex physical features.

Individuals of some species do not live in proximity to others of their species. Sometimes they live so far apart you wonder how males and females find each other. An excellent example of this is deep-sea whales. Whales have a special vocal organ and specially shaped ears able to perceive underwater sounds. The humpback (*Megaptera novaeangliae*) is one of the maestros of the ocean. These whales communicate with members of their species by means of peculiar, far-reaching songs. (Thanks to researchers and modern technology, recordings of these arias are available to the public.)

During the mating season, the serenades of males in the depths of the sea attract female whales from a distance of over sixty miles! The song of these whales, which lasts from five to thirty seconds, is one of the most complex calls in the animal kingdom. Some parts of it are refrains. These songs consist of a series of mumblings, drawling bellows, and moans interrupted by sigh-like sounds, twitters, and screams. They constantly change; the singer modifies some parts with new motifs. The pieces are not just variations of one tune; they differ from each other just as Beethoven differs from the Beatles. The bridal song consists of cyclically recurring scales and is composed according to twelve rules of composition. The female-alluring aria of a lonely male can last as long as twenty-four hours.

The whales' exact method of sound production is mysterious because air is not released into the water (i.e., no bubbles rise to the surface). It seems that during sound production, air flows through an intricate system of tubular cavities in the head of the whale. In other words, the head functions as a huge amplifier.

Communication between humpbacks is indispensable for whales to find each other for coupling. It is quite complicated, for it is not enough to emit the sound; it has to be heard as well. Whales have a very specialized ear

that makes underwater directional hearing possible.

Terrestrial animals are able to determine the direction of the sound source because the stimulus coming from the source reaches their two ears at two slightly different points in time. This does not happen underwater because sound vibrations, due to the excellent sound conducting properties of water, travel almost simultaneously to the cranial bones. Terrestrial animals hear incoming underwater sound vibrations in both ears almost at the same time. (That is why it is difficult for humans to determine the direction of the source of sounds heard underwater.) But whales, having perfect stereophonic hearing, are able to tell the direction from which sounds originate under water because the bony part of their ear is bound to the skull through connective tissue. Therefore their small bony auditory structures (ossicles) can freely vibrate, and do not transmit the vibrations directly to the cranial bone. The design of the auditory ossicles of the inner ear (the malleus, incus, and stapes, also known as the hammer, anvil, and stirrup) also facilitates hearing distant sound. We can compare their auditory system to a sensitive seismograph with which geologists register remote seismic waves.

According to the current theory about the origin of whales, these huge water mammals evolved to aquatic creatures from terrestrial mammals. The perfectly designed ultrasound generator and receiver of humpbacks alone prompts us to question this—the anatomical structure of their organ of hearing being completely different from that of terrestrials. Other observations also seem to indicate that they appeared independently of terrestrial mammals. For example, whales are all born tail first because if the baby whale's head came out first, it would drown by the time its mother completed the delivery. Terrestrial animals are all born headfirst, otherwise their legs would obstruct their coming out. If animals born with their heads first had moved into the seas, their young would have drowned at birth.

Additionally, the nipples of female whales are in a pouch so they don't interfere with the body's streamlined shape. Their skin over the entire body surface is made of a very energy-efficient material that enhances their ability to move through water without resistance. Whales are also champions of immersion. Certain species can dive as deep as 10,000 feet. At 3,500 feet, the pressure is already 101 atmospheres. To avoid having this tremendous pressure collapse their lungs and constrict their respiratory tracts, cartilaginous rings support even the smallest bronchioles. For us, diving to such depths would be fatal; the increasing pressure would dissolve more and more air (mostly nitrogen) from the lungs into the blood. By surfacing too quickly, gases dissolved in the blood produce bubbles that clog the veins and may cause death by embolism. To avoid this phenomenon called caisson disease, diver's paralysis, or the bends, divers must rise to the surface slowly and gradually or adjust to the outer air pressure in pressure-reducing chambers. Whales do not need to do this. They have many more alveoli (air-containing cells in their lungs), and their blood contains 1.5 times more hemoglobin than that of humans. The oxygen-storing capacity of their muscles and tissues is extremely high. Thus they can stay deep under the water for more than an hour with a single inhalation. Diving into the depths, their heart beats half as much as normal. They are also able to exclude blood circulation to non-essential parts of their body. Their nose is also very specialized; it is uniquely located on the top of their head and closed with a strong ring-like muscle.

The anatomical structure, biological function, and way of life of whales are so distinctly different from those of terrestrial mammals that they cannot possibly have evolved from the latter by small genetic changes; aquatics require the simultaneous presence of all their complex features to survive. Perfect acoustical and other constructions are required for their serenades and way of life in the vastness of the ocean; they could only exist from a detailed preliminary plan.

Employing sounds to allure their mates has another interesting feature, considering the entirety of the animal kingdom. Although each species emits sound signals that resemble signals of other species, the animals never mistake the sounds for those of another species. Partners react only to signals from the same species. For example, the call by males of most frog species is standard but species-specific in terms of pitch and timing. Females obey only the call of their own species. The females of many frog species have numerous receptor cells in the ear that are sensitive only to the frequency of the voice of males belonging to the same species. They hardly have any other cells able to receive other wavelengths and are practically deaf to the voice of males of other species. Such harmony between sounds and sound-receiving organs likewise presupposes the previously mentioned requirement of simultaneous appearance, while excluding the possibility of gradual evolution.

Tuned to one scent

Besides communicating with sounds, another way of alluring a prospective "spouse" from great distances is the use of chemical scents, called pheromones. Many animals use this method. One of them is the silk moth (*Bombyx mori*). The female moth lures the male to her from a distance of a few miles by means of a sexual pheromone called bombykol. The male, despite thousands of other scents flowing in the air, detects the moth perfume—because the organ of smell on its antennas is sensitive only to this one compound! Thus it is highly sensitive to this one scent. Researchers of this field made a remarkable calculation. Let us imagine that we mix twenty gallons of moth-alluring bombykol with the water of all the seas on Earth. We would get a huge amount of an extremely thin solution. If we put just one drop of this sexual pheromone cocktail near the organ of smell of the male insect, it would immediately detect the scent of the female!

This great sensitivity is due to the fact that the molecular surface of the chemical sense organ on the antenna of the silk moth is in conformity with the structure and shape of bombykol scent molecules! The surface membrane of nerve endings is microscopically shaped in such a way that the special scent (and only that) may link to it. They fit into each other like a key fits into a lock. (On the other hand, the female moth is completely insensitive to chemical stimuli; one might say that she is "blind" to scent.)

Sexual pheromones of similar insect species often differ from one another only very slightly (e.g., the exact place of a

104

The meeting of the two sexes of a species is possible because the calling sounds and the sound-receiving organs are tuned to each other.

Calling sounds of male frogs are species specific. Females respond only to signals emitted by a member of their own species.

protruding atomic group). Thus scent molecules link up with the receptors very precisely. Nature's intelligence achieves this so that males of different insect species are attracted to females of their own species only.

Let us try to investigate where scent-message systems (which initially may seem simple but in reality are very complex) come from. First we have to know that sexual pheromones are produced by exocrine glands, and the discharge of a certain composition gets to the outside world through separate outlet tubes. In the bodies of bees and ants, for example, there are more than ten kinds of exocrine glands, the discharges of which get to different parts of their body through small ducts. It is not possible to explain the origin of this complex system of hormones and the resultant chemical messaging as the result of evolution. The accidental and gradual appearance of glands of differing functions, equipped with the appropriate small tubes to disseminate various chemicals, is highly improbable.

Besides this, there are many other discrepancies. If the one-time ancestor of the silk moth did not have this alluring scent, how would the male have found its mate? How would the species have survived? It is especially remarkable that scent molecules emitted by the female (those and only those) fit exactly into the male's receptor. There is no possibility of repeated attempts or "adaptation through thousands of years." The sexual pheromone sent out is either perfectly attuned to the receptor "moth nose," or the relationship of sexes cannot take place; thus the species dies off. Ideas of a step-by-step evolution through thousands of years do not make sense. The chances are practically impossible that, by an accidental genetic mutation, a female emerged that produced the exact bombykol formula, and at the same time, by mere chance, a male was born with a receptor that was sensitive exclusively to bombykol.

One may argue that perhaps in the distant past, the female silk moth produced several different compounds, and the male had been able to discern several scents. The method of communication between the two became "restricted" to the use of bombykol only later. But how did this situation, considered the state of origin, emerge? Somehow, they had to find each other even then. In other words, the harmony should have already existed at that time. This assumption does not solve the problem; it only pushes it back in time.

Another possible explanation about the origin of modern silk moths could go something like this: The ancestor of silk moths might have found its mate by some other (non-chemical) method, and

106

Night moths are able to find each other only by scent signals, but even day moths may sometimes depend on smells when looking for a mate.

communication via bombykol developed later. But since the communication system using bombykol can only function if it's complete, it could replace another system only if all the elements of the new system emerged simultaneously. It is inconceivable that the complicated scent-emitting and scent-perceiving systems gradually evolved over thousands of years, without any real benefit, until (following an inauguration ceremony) they started functioning. Mutations and innovations having no benefit for their host disappear, or if they somehow remain, they do not evolve any further into useful organs through many useless steps. Perhaps evolu-

tionists' explanations regarding the origin of chemical communication need to evolve.

To assume that such inventions were originally born in the mind of an intelligent designer, a very imaginative bioengineer, may not seem too bold after all.

Captivating lights

Some nocturnal animals rely on light emission to find a mate. This is generally used by insects, the greater firefly (*Lampyris noctiluca*) being a well-known example.

Its light organ is on the ventral side of the abdomen, and it looks like two greenish-yellow phosphorescent spots in the dark. The phosphorescent spots consist of three main layers of cells. The bottom layer is made of cells full of tiny angular crystals. These crystals return most of the light cast upon them, thus enhancing the phosphorescence of the spots. The actual light cells are in the middle layer. The external layer of the little organ is the skin itself, which is transparent exactly at these places so that the light of the spots is visible. Fireflies generate light in the following way: a protein called luciferin oxidizes in the presence of an enzyme called luciferase. This enzyme is in itself quite complex; it consists of about a thousand amino acid units. The reaction of the two substances generates "cold light," a process called bioluminescence.

Fine branches of the tracheal system densely infiltrate the small, separately innerved organ. By the help of this neat little apparatus, the bug transforms at least ninety percent of the chemical energy into cold light. This is an amazingly effective use of energy if we consider that most light bulbs transform only four percent of the energy conducted into them into light and waste ninety-six percent of it in the form of heat. Man-made light bulbs are less efficient than the light bulbs in fireflies!

Several firefly species live in the tropics, and all of them find other members of the same species by emitting light signals. The frequency of the signals is species-specific. The female waiting on the ground responds to light signals of a flying male flashed at a given frequency by flashing her light source at regular intervals. The male does not respond to signals by related species, only to those of a female belonging to its own species.

The light of the firefly illuminates the fact that the animal kingdom is full of systems of sexual communication that could not have evolved by accident in a gradual way. Even with Luciferian logic, it is impossible to explain the cooperation of luciferin and luciferase and the extremely effective and accurate little lamp at the end of the bug's abdomen, to which a wonderful light-reflecting layer, a complex neural control, and an ability of intraspecific time pattern recognition are associated. Such things cannot happen by chance. The firefly is proof of something—or someone—else.

The chase is better than the catch

After males and females find each other, pre-mating courting begins. For some animals the impressive courting behavior is short and

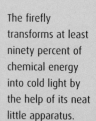

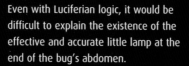

The firefly transforms at least ninety percent of chemical energy into cold light by the help of its neat little apparatus.

Even with Luciferian logic, it would be difficult to explain the existence of the effective and accurate little lamp at the end of the bug's abdomen.

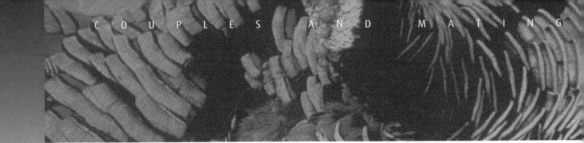

The males of many species try to draw attention to themselves by the help of eye-catching feathers. Is the peacock's display a result of natural selection or conscious design?

superficial, and for others it is longer and sometimes intense and complicated. Males of several species try to draw attention to themselves with brilliant feathers or vivid spots, which they display repeatedly during their courting rituals. Females usually mate with the most decorative and strongest male, the one whose looks and performance are the most convincing to them.

Members of some species work hard to catch the attention of their prospective partners by alluring movements or even by a complicated "show," a whole mating parade. In certain animals, the glaring, eye-catching colors or stimulatory scents appear only during their mating period. For example, at the time of spawning, the abdomen of the three-spined stickleback (*Gasterosteus aculeatus*) male, a fish living by the shores of Europe and North America, becomes bright red, and his eyes become blue.

Roe hills at the bottom of the lake

Males of certain species draw attention to themselves by altering their environment in an extreme way. In the Malawi Lake in

The knowledge of satin bowerbirds is complementary: the male knows what to attract the hen with, while the hen knows what to be attracted to.

Central Africa, different species of cichlids (*Cichlidae*) shoal. Their courting habits are perplexing even for zoologists. Males of some species build roe hills on the bottom of the lake, by which they aspire to earn the females' approval. The height of the hills varies from one and a half to six inches, sometimes even higher. The diameter of some stately "sand-castles" can be nearly ten feet. The top of the structures is either flat or concave.

Males belonging to the same species build their nests close to each other. Consequently, females can look at all the hills at once and decide which master builder to choose. If a female takes a liking to a hill, she lays her eggs on it. Cichlids do not abandon their young. They nurse them in different ways: some of them keep the small ones together on the bottom, while others, after their young have hatched from the fertilized roe kept in their mouth, continue to give them shelter in their oral cavity for some time.

Show me your bower!

Males of the eighteen bowerbird species living in New Guinea and the virgin forests of North Australia build not just simple nests, but alluring structures (bowers) showing off their exquisite taste. They decorate their home (made of twigs and branches) with butterfly wings, flowers, feathers, and rags. The female bases her mate selection on the attractiveness of the decorated bower.

Satin bowerbirds (*Ptilonorhynchus violaceus*) also belong to these species. The males build walkways made of two parallel rows of perpendicular sticks, usually orientated in a north-south direction. The male places these twig walls on a tightly woven foundation. A bower most worthy of interest to the female is about a yard wide and thirty inches high. The most fashionable edifices are tightly woven and neat. The inside of the twig walls are daubed over with a mixture of saliva, charcoal, berries, and pigments. Females are sensitive to colors. The favorite color of satin bowerbird hens is blue. The more blue there is in a bower, the more attractive it is to them. The desire to please is so strong in males that sometimes they destroy a competitor's bower and filch the most beautiful ornaments. The number of furnishings can reach a hundred. The most popular trinkets are blue feathers, for which males fight an exciting stealing match. Those who manage to "feather their nests" impress the females more.

If the cock manages to lure the hen by the beauty of the bower, he picks up an ornament, spreads his quill feathers out in a fan-like way, and struts up and down before her while making a booming sound. Mating takes place in about thirty minutes.

Mechanical architects

The architectural art of both cichlids and satin bowerbirds is hereditary. Other members of the animal kingdom are born with a plan in their head, too. Carefully built nests of potter wasps

(*Sceliphron destillatorium*) also are not the result of conscious planning but are exclusively instinctual. The wasp larva grows up alone; it does not learn its architectural ability from anyone. Still it builds its nest meticulously when the time comes. But the steps of its behavior are predetermined; it cannot adjust them to occasional changes of the situation. Some insects construct their buildings through thousands of steps. If they are interrupted or the building is damaged, they are unable to go back a few hundred steps. They continue their work, even if the outcome is a deformed, useless structure. In fact, since they think they have already built the nest, they try to use it later on as if it were ready, although in reality it does not function properly.

The nest of weaverbirds (which hangs down from a branch) is also a result of a long series of operations. But if the finished nest, consisting of an intricate structure of inter-woven blades of grass, gets damaged, the bird is unable to mend it or do the work again from the appropriate working phase. Instead, it destroys the whole thing and starts building it from the very beginning. It is like dance students who know the choreography only from the very beginning, and can only "take it from the top" instead of starting where they left off.

Therefore, these wonderful structures seem to be products of the intellectual abilities of these animals. In reality, we see that they have a rigid, predefined behavior that they are unable to modify, and they can execute only a certain sequence of operations. (Of course, there are animals that are able to think in a more flexible way.) From where does this inherent, compelling course of action come? The structures just mentioned are very complicated. It

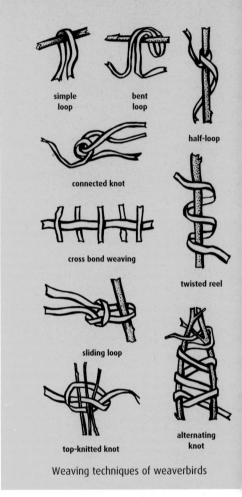

simple loop

bent loop

half-loop

connected knot

cross bond weaving

twisted reel

sliding loop

top-knitted knot

alternating knot

Weaving techniques of weaverbirds

is hard to believe that the builders developed the skill to build them over thousands or millions of years, slowly progressing from building only a foundation or putting a few straws in place up to the present complex creations. Unfinished or partly built structures are useless and completely inadequate for further mutational development. If the animals did not invent them, then chance alone could not have catalyzed the animals to build them. Only an intelligent designer could invent such structures.

Although weaverbirds make their nests in a very complicated way, they simply obey a series of instincts programmed into them. They are unable to revise or modify the "program."

We have learned that the knowledge possessed by males and females of the same species is in perfect sync. One party knows how to attract the other, and the other party knows what it is supposed to respond to. Without these matching and complementing instincts, reproduction could not take place. The behavior of the male satin bowerbirds fulfills exactly the expectations of the hens. Instincts of the two sexes must have appeared at the same time, tuned to each other.

The origin of sexual characteristics

According to the evolutionist philosophy, conspicuous sexual characteristics (the vivid colors and patterns of males, their eye-catching behavior) developed via the evolutionary process. Traits of successful males quickly proliferated and became more and more prevalent in the population. Adepts of this view propose that the imposing courting behavior of peacocks, displaying their huge tail feathers, developed because the hens favored this particular variety of behavior and tail feathers as the most attractive for a mate to have.

But we have seen that the mating behavior of many species, with the two sexes keenly tuned to each other's very subtle characteristics, is so complex that the gradual development theory trips on the very first steps. We may rightly suppose that different conspicuous colors, patterns, and courting behaviors did not develop by selection; they are inherent aspects ensuring the successful attraction and reproduction of the sexes. Males have appropriate looks and instincts to command the attention of females, whose senses are "sharpened" to signals meant for them. In other words, males have always tried to dazzle females and induce them to mate. And the decision of females preserves rather than changes the species-specific traits of the males.

Dance and presents

In many species, dance is an integral part of the relationship of sexes. Sometimes males cut a dashing figure, and females passively

It is probable that eye-catching colors and courting behaviors did not evolve through selection but have always existed to ensure that each of the two sexes finds one another for successful mating.

watch. Other species perform their mating dance in a duet.

The brownish-white winter plumage of great crested grebes (*Podiceps cristatus*) changes to more vivid colors in spring. Grebes seal their mate selection for life by synchronized swimming in couples. The nuptial dance is a way to ascertain their partner's health, coordinating abilities, and physical condition. At first, one of them swims underwater toward the other while the latter is watching in a characteristic bent posture. Then the bird swimming emerges from under the water in a vertical position and both of them begin to shake their heads and arrange each other's wing feathers. Out of the many similar, highly elaborate scenes, the most lyrical is the "hair-weed dance" directly preceding nesting. They both dive under the water and emerge with a bunch of hair-weed in their bills. Then they quickly swim toward each other swaying their heads, and completely emerging from the water, start dancing.

How is it possible that two birds of the opposite sex know the exact sequence of dance steps one after another and react according to the movements of their partner? In the evolutionist view, all this is the result of "ritualization," a process by which eating and

Great crested grebes seal their mate selection by a water ballet. They do not need to practice the choreography; they know it immediately—but from where?

washing movements develop into a ritual. This superficial statement does not at all answer the how-and-why of its development; nor does it answer the question of the origin of the sequence of movements and the mystery of the mutual understanding of the movements.

In addition to wedding dances, the males of some species also bring wedding presents. In many spider species, the male shrinks into insignificance beside the threateningly huge female. It can easily happen that the female mistakes the "gentleman" approaching her to become a husband and father as prey and devours him instead. Thus, males wanting to mate have to approach the females very carefully. For the "stalking," different species use different tactics. Some males start struggling and kicking with their legs, while others distinguish themselves from insect-prey by complicated dance steps on entering the female's web. Still others apply the method of "appeasement": they bring delicious tidbits (insects) as presents for the female. But this is

not a completely selfless donation. While the female is busy eating, they perform the fertilization.

In all cases, the male spider has to be aware that he is smaller and know what to do so the female does not eat him. Without this knowledge, spiders would soon become extinct. Since spiders exist, this kind of behavior has to exist, too. If at any point in time, the behavior had been incomplete or missing, the male would have inevitably perished even before mating. The male and

The courting of European bee-eaters includes the giving of an insect as a gift, followed by mating.

Their nest is an egg chamber without lining, dug into a sandy or loamy deposit.

After mating, the female praying mantis often eats the much smaller male.

The male raft spider is also smaller than the female.

the female both have to know the "password"—the only possibility for the prospective spider-father to stay alive. It is worth noting that the tarantula (*Lycosa tarentula*) male even has two hooks on his forefeet used to hold the female down while mating and keep clear of her life-threatening fangs.

A delicate subject

The most important, indispensable circumstance needed for reproduction is mating itself. In the animal world, genitals of the opposite sexes fit exactly with each other, just like a key fits into its corresponding lock. Let us consider, for example, insects. Genitals of the different species are of differing shapes and structure, but they consist of rather simple chitinous appendages. With a little exaggeration, we may say that nearly all species have more or less differing genital organs, which, in the majority of cases, makes mating of insects belonging to different species impossible. This wonderfully species-specific interlocking of genitals seriously questions the possibility of development by evolution. Let us take into

consideration that in case of a supposed step-by-step development, the appropriate organs of the male and female would have changed many, many times in both sexes at the same time, in a way that they still exactly fit with each other. This is simply absurd.

Out of respect for our more conservative readers, we will not mention any more graphic examples in connection with this topic. Let us instead consider two special ways of reproduction, which also support our basic assumption.

Scorpion waltzer

Scorpions are able to paralyze the heart action and respiratory muscles of their victim with their stinger, which stands out at the end of their curling metasoma ("tail"). These animals, wary of each other, even go about mating

The male tarantula has two hooks on his forefeet in order to keep off the female's life-threatening fangs while mating. The complexities of the behavior and physical structure mutually suppose each other; they could not have evolved step by step.

has to release it and drag the female above it. Also, it would be pointless to have the hereditary ability to make the female dance in the appropriate direction if his spermatophore did not have these special technical features.

The possibility of this method of reproduction developing step by step, via small genetic mutations, is practically unimaginable. Because of the complexity of behavior and

Yellow fattail scorpions would not be able to reproduce if their mating behavior did not completely fit their complicated anatomy.

very cautiously. The male and female yellow fattail scorpions (*Androc tonus australis*) first viciously grab each other's pincers to neutralize the weapon of their partner. Next they curl up their tail so that it does not hamper them, and then begin to "dance" by trotting right and left. The purpose of the waltzers soon becomes clear. After a certain time, the male draws the female near him, while he drops a spermatophore equipped with an ejecting system (possessing "hooks" and "springs") on the ground. Then he works hard to drag his mate above it. When the sexual slit of the female is exactly above the spermatophore, the hooks clasp into it, the "springs" release, and the spermatophore penetrates the female's body. The fertilized female later retires to lay her eggs.

The scorpion's complicated and very precise organic construction complements its hereditary reproductive behavior. The spring-loaded structure of the seed-carrying spermatophore of the male, which is exactly suitable for carrying out the reproductive process, activates when the female reaches the appropriate place above it. The male's well-timed behavior supports this technological perfection. At the right moment, he releases the packet and drags his mate above it. If any part of the process was missing, scorpions could not reproduce. It would be useless for the male to have a special spermatophore if he did not know when he

116

The mating of dragonflies involves real aerobatics. Still, they know exactly how to act, even without any sex education.

organic construction needed, the whole of the series of actions is useful only if all its elements and accessories are in place. The alternative scenario, which envisions the whole system evolving by a single accidental mutation from living beings reproducing in a completely different way, has utterly no chance. It seems that not only the poison of scorpions can be fatal, but their way of reproduction also—at least to the evolutionist view, which excludes higher planning.

The champions of timing

The perfect synchrony of the courting activities of males and females is extremely important in species that reproduce by external fertilization. Since eggs and spermatozoa meet outside the body, they have to be released at the same time; otherwise they would disperse even before fertilization.

To make the next example understandable, we have to say a few words about the movements of the sea. The sea level rises and sinks twice every day. Six hours pass between each ebb and flow. Due to the movement of planets and the gravitational pull between them, the extent of the fall between ebb and flow changes cyclically. The highest flow and the lowest ebb take place when the earth, the sun, and the moon are in line. In geography, this is called tidal wave. (Everyday language and the media inaccurately use this term for an extremely destructive, sweeping, huge wall of water caused by volcanic eruptions or earthquakes; the proper name for this is tsunami, which is a phenomenon independent of the cyclical movements of the sea.) Tidal wave, when the flow is highest, occurs twice a month.

On full-moon nights in March (at the time of the biggest difference in the level of the ebb and flow) on the Pacific coasts of Southern California, there are millions of silvery lustrous-bodied Californian grunions (*Lauresthes tenuis*). These small fish voluntarily throw themselves ashore in the tidal zone, as far as the eye can see along the coast. Each coming wave spreads a new mass of floundering little fish on the coast. When they get ashore, females quickly dig themselves into the sand with wriggling movements, flouncing with their caudal fin. They get into a vertical position, until only their head sticks out of the sand. Each male chooses himself a mate, and coiling around her, he discharges his sperm while the female lays her eggs into the sand. The next wave carries the pairs back into the sea.

In the next few days, the ocean recedes and the fertilized roes can lay undisturbed in the wet sand for two weeks, where sea predators cannot snatch them. Finally, the next tidal wave (the highest flow), rising due to the added gravitation of the sun and the moon, again inundates the seashore. The waves rumbling over the roe in the sand of the spawning ground release the fries from them, which then begin their life in the ocean. (The only drawback of this form of reproduction is that some of the fish throwing themselves ashore, as well as some of the roe and the hatching fries, fall victim to seagulls.)

Because of the strict timing, the reproduction of Californian grunions has to be quite concerted. At an appropriate point of the ebb and flow cycle, members of both sexes have to work hard to beach themselves (which, since they are fish, is surprising enough). They need the adequate instincts to play their precise role during the short time spent in the sand. The period of the roes' development also exactly corresponds with the cycle of the ocean's movements. They begin to develop during one tidal wave, and the next one finds them ready for life in the water. Thus their parents conceive them between two waves of

The many ways that individuals of the opposite sex find each other and mate cause as much confusion to scientists as the animals' behaviors of self-sustenance.

the ocean, and their development takes place between two tidal waves.

How can we interpret their reproduction as anything other than a perfect, inseparable, unified system? Fish "evolving to the seashore" at the wrong time and place, lacking knowledge of the required action could by no means survive. The most probable explanation for their origin is that they appeared in the ocean already in possession of their unique method of reproduction, as we know it today.

Specific reproductions

The examples cited above give us an idea of the major factors that play a part in an animal finding a mate and reproducing. Animals find or lure their mates with the help of sounds, scents, light signals, and sometimes by alluring movements. The vivid, conspicuous sexual characteristics, special colors, spots, or

feathers of some animals also play a part in the shaping of their sexual behavior. Males of certain species try to draw the attention of females by impo-

sing postures, an impressive series of actions, or sometimes by stately structures. A courting dance or giving presents may also precede mating. Matching sexual organs and adequate postures and behaviors are required for successful mating. In certain examples, even timing plays a crucial part.

Naturally, we do not find all the phases in each species; the modes of courting and mating vary. Sometimes one feature becomes dominant, sometimes another. But it is common in all species that besides the adequate anatomical traits, individuals must have a strictly determined race-preserving instinct, matching the behavior of the individual of the opposite sex. The origin of these traits is rather puzzling. As we have seen from the examples in this chapter, their gradual development is most improbable. It is presumable that the same superior being provided all living beings with the appropriate inner urges and physical features for reproduction. It is as if this being had intended for each existing species to ensure the existence of offspring similar to them by reproducing in a specific way, characteristic only of them. Why is this of interest to the designer of brilliant intelligence? We will answer this in detail in the last chapter.

The new generation

The New Generation

After individuals of two sexes from the same species successfully find each other and mate, the fertilized eggs begin to develop. Let us see, through several examples, how members of the next generation mature. Numerous extraordinary cases present a great challenge to biologists who still think according to the evolutionist paradigm.

120

By nature's wise arrangement, those species that leave their offspring to their own devices following birth, or sometimes right after conception, bring a great number of issues to the world; many of these offspring die. Conversely, those that give birth to few issues protect them with great care.

It is also part of nature's order that animal species (thanks to their race-preserving instinct) ensure the security of their eggs and the conditions for the initial development of their offspring in a way appropriate for their species. Newborns and growing members of the animal kingdom are usually exposed to many dangers until they reach (if they reach) adulthood. Parents protect juveniles from most of these dangers. This we take for granted. Where did the parent animals' comprehensive instincts for proliferation and nurturing offspring come from?

Species that give birth to few offspring, such as red-headed vultures, take care of their young with great attention.

Most frog species lay eggs. Tadpoles hatch in the water from these eggs and gradually develop into full-grown frogs.

Birds know how to ensure the security of their eggs and how to bring up and protect their fledglings, thanks to their regulated race-preserving instinct.

121

Frog babies and frog midwives

Let us first visit the world of frogs. The reproduction of frogs can only take place in water; it is an indispensable habitat for rearing their young as well. Most frog species reproduce and care for their offspring by a similar process. First they lay eggs, and from the eggs, tadpoles hatch (this is called the "larval stage"). The tadpoles gradually lose their tails, grow limbs, and (after many other anatomical changes) become frogs. Tadpoles of most species transform into frogs in water, but sometimes it is not such an easy task to ensure a proper environment for them. Some frog species solve this problem in quite extraordinary ways.

The midwife toad (*Alytes obstetricans*), living in Europe, spends most of its time in holes on the banks of lakes and rivers. It mates on land. When the female lays her eggs, the male fertilizes them. After fifteen minutes, the male picks up the chains of eggs and fixes them on his hind thigh. The following few weeks, he wanders here and there like this, and if he finds the environment too dry, he looks for wetter regions. When it's time for the eggs to hatch, the frog jumps into a lake or river. He remains in the water for an hour or so, until all the tadpoles hatch. Then he returns to his own hole.

South American poison dart frogs (e.g., golden poison dart frogs, *Dendrobates auratus*) use a similarly artful technique. They lay their eggs in a wet place; then the male cuddles up to them to guard them. When the eggs hatch, the tadpoles immediately flounder to the male and crawl on his back. The skin of the father's back excretes mucus in great quantities, and the young can escape from drying out only by sticking to it. The male carries them to a nearby lake and dives into the water. The layer of mucus on his back dissolves, and the tadpoles slip into the water and start their independent life. One more interesting element in this

Those animals that have a large number of issues (ladybugs, for instance) usually leave them to their own devices.

The male of the poison dart frog guards the eggs. Hatching tadpoles instinctively climb on their father's sticky back to get to the nearest pond.

situation is that tadpoles of poison dart frogs, unlike those of other species, have no gills; they absorb oxygen through the skin of their body and enlarged tail. It is also notable that the young are immune from the strong poison on the back of the male.

The South American marsupial frog (*Gastrotheca ovifera*) performs one of the most extraordinary and physically complicated reproductive techniques. This procedure requires

Young poison dart frogs are immune from the poisonous skin of the male. If it were not so, they would immediately die. Where does this chemical harmony come from?

that the eggs and developing tadpoles remain in the body of one of the parents, since this is what ensures their necessary humidity. The female has a large pouch on her back with an orifice on it. When the mating begins, the male, which is much smaller than the female, mounts on her back and holds on to her neck. The female lifts her hind legs, and curving her back and pressing her nose to the ground, presses out the eggs from within one by one. After the male fertilizes them, the eggs roll along a slimy path and enter the large pouch of the female. They stay in the "hatching bag" until fully developed. The female releases them from the bag by stretching her hind leg forward and sticking her longest toe into the orifice of the pouch. The small frogs

creep forth through the enlarged orifice. This frog species does not have a tadpole form during its development! Several forest-dwelling frogs develop entirely within the egg, and in certain species, organs characteristic of tadpoles do not even appear. The small frogs come out of the eggs in their fully developed form.

A species called Darwin's frogs (*Rhinoderma darwinii*) exhibits the most bizarre variety of such "bearing methods." Darwin himself discovered this tiny frog in Chile. After female Darwin's frogs lay their eggs on wet beaches, males sense the scent of the eggs and fertilize them. They then station themselves beside the eggs in groups and guard them for about twenty days. When the developing eggs begin to move in their tiny, jelly-like globules, the males lean over to them and gulp—they seemingly eat them! Of course, they do not eat the eggs but instead place them with their tongue into their long

expandable vocal pouch, situated in the lower part of their body. The eggs continue to develop in the vocal pouch until one day the male suddenly yawns widely, and the fully developed baby frogs jump out of his mouth.

In each of the cases above, frog parents protect the eggs from desiccation in very special ways. We run into serious difficulties if we try to explain the origin of developmental peculiarities of these frogs based on the theory of evolution. We see hereditary behavior in all four of them, combined with specific physical structures. Let us see how complex they are through the example of Darwin's frog.

For viable offspring to hatch, the frog father must know that he has to keep an eye on the eggs. Furthermore, he has to have the instincts commanding the right behavior: when the young are about to hatch, he has to get them into his specially structured vocal pouch. And when they are fully developed, he has to set them free. If any of these elements were missing, the frog's reproduction would be unsuccessful. Therefore it is inconceivable that the Darwin's frog and its special way of reproduction came into existence step by step, as a result of small changes.

Naturally, the vocal pouch has a role in the frog's communication, too, but there is no logical explanation as to what would have made a frog, which in theory used to proliferate in a different way, change its behavior to guard the eggs' development by putting them in his vocal pouch at the right time.

Current knowledge systems describe the behavior of living beings as governed by complex genetic programs, transmitted in the DNA of individuals. It is inconceivable that this frog species, with its specialized behavior, came into existence by a sudden large-scale mutation. In commanding the reproductive behaviors and forms of parental care mentioned above, there are certainly countless genetic units playing a part, which, moreover, are isolated from each other in the genetic material. The chance mutation of these genes causing a series of concerted, appropriate behaviors would be more than a miracle. On

Young marsupial frogs develop in a large pouch on their mother's back, from which they emerge only when they look almost exactly like their parents. The idea is original, but what is its origin?

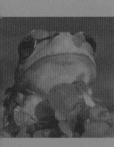

the other hand, we can discard the possibility of gradual development, because all the elements of the behavior (guarding the eggs, taking them into the mouth, putting them into the bag, releasing them) have to be present at the same time so that the species can reproduce at all. Thus, in future textbooks, this frog should appear under the name "Anti-Darwin frog" (*Rhinoderma antidarwinii*).

As we have seen, frogs living in different conditions have different (sometimes quite unique) methods of race preservation. These methods differ from each other in both anatomical and behavioral aspects, and it is impossible to trace one back to the other. Each reproductive system works perfectly in its complexity, but if only one element is missing or changed, the entire system would stop functioning altogether. Moreover, because the anatomical construction of animals must always be in harmony with their behavior, we should also suppose that whenever the anatomy of animals changed (because of accidental genetic mutations) simultaneously there would have to be equivalent accidental behavioral mutations causing them to behave in accordance with their new physical structure. Since the probability of such a constant coincidence of accidents is infinitesimal, it is simpler to acknowledge that the reproductive methods of frogs have always been—and will always remain—unchanging but species specific.

Born in food

Many species require strictly determined conditions for the young to be born. In such cases the parents behave in precise ways to ensure the successful hatching of their offspring. This behavior is visible in more simple beings such as insects, which, unlike humans, are obviously not able to consider what their young need for development. Their instincts prompt them to act in the proper way. For instance, food is a significant challenge for survival of the unprotected young in the first days of their life. They are sure to survive if the eggs are near or on top of some food. For example, one type of caterpillar hatches from eggs put on cabbage leaves and begins to feed directly on the leaves. Species of another insect group called ichneumonids (different chalcid wasps, braconid wasps, fairyflies, ichneumon wasps, and parasitic flies) develop in the grubs and pupas of other bugs, and feed on them.

The larvae of a large ichneumon wasp (*Rhyssa persuasoria*), for instance, kill young wood-wasps. To do this, the female ichneumon wasp first has to find the larva of the wood-wasp. The ichneumon feels the bark of trees with her antennules, and when she perceives the fine vibrations made by the larva of the wood-wasp, she takes action. She lifts her abdomen high and holds her narrow ovipositor, which is almost as long as the wasp itself, in ready repose, boring it into the wood where the larva of the wood-wasp develops, one inch deep. When the tip of the ovipositor reaches the victim, the female lays an egg on the larva or beside it. The larva of the ichneumon wasp hatching out of the egg devours the larva of the wood-wasp, and then spins a cocoon around itself, from which the fully developed ichneumon wasp will hatch later on.

The ichneumon wasp's way of living and style of reproducing is in harmony with its special "tool," the ovipositor. It is doubtful that without an original, designing intelligence, such an expedient and efficient behavior could have developed. The female of the ichneumon

Reptiles and birds have to ensure the right temperature for their eggs to hatch.

125

wasp must know what she is looking for, how she can find it, and once she finds it, what exactly she should do. Without this instinctive action, members of this species could not reproduce in the present, nor could they have survived in the past.

Nature's thermostat

For young reptiles and birds to be born, their parents have to ensure exactly the right temperature for the eggs to hatch. The East Australian mallee fowl (*Leipoa ocellata*) employs a "living thermostat" in its reproductive process. It creates a huge incubator-like nest mound, regularly checks the ground temperature, and immediately corrects it if it deviates by more than 1.8 degrees Fahrenheit from the ideal temperature.

First, mallee fowl parents dig a hole fifteen feet wide and three feet deep. During wintertime, they gather twigs and leaves from within a radius of fifty yards and amass them in the hole. When the material thus gathered gets thoroughly soaked in the rain, they cover the whole thing with a layer of sandy earth twenty inches thick. This is how the mallee

If any element of the complex hatching method of mallee fowl had been missing in the past, they would not have been able to hatch their eggs.

builds its crater-like nest, which towers nearly five feet high; the volume of the nest can be as much as forty cubic yards.

The mallee fowl lays her eggs on rotting leaves in the egg chamber within the nest mound. The male first checks whether conditions are appropriate and lets the female lay the eggs only afterward. When the female comes out, the male buries the egg chamber. Starting in the spring, for three to four months, the hen comes once a week, lays one egg each time, and always entrusts the castle to the care of her mate. The incubation period is very long. The cock takes care of the right incubation temperature for nine months.

The eggs hatch due to the warmth of the hill. The male sticks his bill into the hill from time to time to check the temperature of the soil. He is able to measure the exact temperature most probably with his tongue or oral cavity. Functioning as an incubator, he maintains the temperature of the mound at 93.2 degrees Fahrenheit with incredible precision. He allows a maximum fluctuation of 1.8 degrees, although in that region daily and yearly temperatures vary considerably.

In spring, when rotting vegetable matter generates heat from which the eggs could overheat, he assiduously removes the sand from the top of the hill to dissipate the extra heat. In summer, the mound has to be protected from excessive sunshine; under such circumstances he scratches more soil onto the mound lest the sunshine overheat the nest. And in fall, when the outside weather turns colder and the inside heat emanating from rotting vegetation also decreases, he removes the upper layers of the hill during the day so that the sun shines right on the middle of the nest and warms the eggs. By night he again covers them to retain the heat. Amazingly, the mallee fowl is able to forecast the weather; he

often makes the necessary changes in the nest mound a few hours beforehand, in anticipation of weather changes.

Hatching chicks dig themselves out of the mound at different times and immediately leave the "family nest." They learn from no one how to build a mound and how to maintain its temperature. Still, when they "come of age," they behave exactly as their parents did.

The example of this bird species alone counters any theory of evolution. It is incomprehensible that the mallee fowl could have evolved from any other bird, either by gradual changes or by a one-time mutation. Its extraordinary heat sensing is in itself sensational, and the thoroughness of the bird's entire nesting behavior makes its characteristics all the more remarkable. It builds a special nest mound at the right time, gathers vegetable matter, and heaps sand on top of it. The male possesses the appropriate knowledge and behavioral mechanisms to correct the fluctuation of temperature inside the mound, not to mention his weather forecasting abilities.

The gradual evolution of the mallee fowl is not possible. The birds' whole way of living and method of hatching has a meaning only if each mosaic of its behavior is in its proper place. If any of the elements were missing (e.g., the heat-sensing organ, the science of how to build a mound, or the knowledge of what is to be done in case of fluctuations in temperature), the bird could not hatch the eggs. And evolution by a one-time mutation (i.e., for a bird that hatched in a totally different way to suddenly have had a mallee fowl nestling) is also impossible because of the incredible complexity involved.

The mallee fowl is the paragon of fatherly care. The most rational explanation of the origin of this bird, equipped with the impulses

Eggs of cuckoos look just like those of the host birds. This must have always been; otherwise songbirds would have removed cuckoo eggs—and thus the cuckoo species—from the nest forever.

this is especially important, because they do not build a nest, but smuggle their eggs into other birds' nests. Therefore, they have to look exactly like those of the selected foster mother. Otherwise, the foster mother bird would throw them out. Although cuckoos are capable of laying eggs of amazingly different patterns, each female is capable of laying only one kind. In all likelihood, they inherit the pattern of the egg from their mother and select the right nest by trying to find the same bird species that brought them up.

Is it possible cuckoos' eggs "gradually adapted" to those of songbirds? This is utterly unthinkable because the mother birds would have destroyed eggs of just a little different color and pattern. It is much more probable that the different species-specialist cuckoos appeared together with the songbirds in the distant past. Moreover, one could not tell their eggs from those of their foster parents, and they already knew which songbird's nest they had to approach.

Nile monitors often lay their eggs into a termite hill, and then abandon them. The temperature of the termite hill is ideal for the hatching of the young monitors. But how do monitors know this?

necessary for successful hatching, the heat-sensing organ, and its complex abilities of regulating heat, is that this species was created by a very innovative and meticulous fatherly intelligence.

Cuckoo eggs

The color and pattern of birds' eggs are a result of pigments that deposit on the eggshell while still inside the female's body.

The color and pattern of the eggs of songbirds differ from each other. For the songbird species cuckoos (*Cuculus canorus*),

Cuckoos lay their egg into nests of songbirds such as the warbler, shown here with its own fledglings.

128

Although the less than a half-inch long wallaroo embryo is still blind and deaf, it resolutely climbs toward the pouch. How does it know exactly where to go?

The best guru is the kangaroo

Marsupials—among others, kangaroos—give birth to undeveloped embryo-like offspring that finish their development in their mothers' pouch. Female marsupials, mostly living in Australia (unlike mammals living in other parts of the world), do not have any placenta (a shell enclosing the embryo and ensuring nutriments). Thus, the marsupial embryo gets its nutriment not from the placenta but absorbs it from the wall of the uterus. The embryo stays only a few weeks in the womb. Before delivery, the female kangaroo cleanses the inside of her pouch and the periphery of her sexual slit with her tongue for hours in order to make the way smooth for her newborn. Since the offspring is very small, the delivery is not very difficult for the female.

The baby wallaroo (*Macropus giganteus*) is less than a half-inch long when it comes into

the world and 12,000 times lighter than its 3.2-foot tall mother, in whose womb it spends only five weeks. After its birth, it has to climb about six inches to get into its mother's pouch and find one of the four dugs (udders) from which it will feed during the next one and a half years. The tiny blind embryo instinctively starts toward the protecting and nourishing pouch; it fights its way through its mother's dense fur by pulling itself with its rudimentary front legs. We do not have precise information on exactly how it finds its mother's dug. Since at that time it is completely blind, possibly scents guide it.

Most newborn kangaroos find the dug after three minutes of toilsome travel. Death awaits the ones that do not succeed. Upon reaching its destination, the embryo tightly

clings to the swollen dug, which fits perfectly into its mouth. After only one month, the jaw area of the young kangaroo develops enough for the baby to let go of the dug from time to time. It leaves the pouch at the age of seven months for the first time, and at eleven months up to the age of eighteen months, it lives outside, returning only to feed on its mother's milk. By this time a new embryo is already developing inside her pouch.

The reproduction of marsupial animals is a finely tuned system. Can we really attribute it to natural selection? Kangaroos can only survive if the embryo, which practically looks like a worm, "knows" perfectly what it has to do, i.e., its instincts prompt it to immediately head for the pouch after coming out of the womb. Even though it is blind, it must have the necessary abilities of perception and orientation and be able to find its mother's dug, which is vital for its survival. If, during the imagined evolution of kangaroos, these abilities had not been present, the young would not have survived, and kangaroos would not exist today. Their presence proves that the countless kangaroo ancestors (which looked and behaved the same as the ones today) also had been able to accomplish this extraordinary feat. Another illuminating question is: How would the ontogeny (development) of mammals lacking a placenta have taken place if at some point in time they had not had a pouch? The pouch and the behavior of the embryo are of use only in their interdependence; separately they are useless.

The step-by-step evolution of the growing process and physical traits of kangaroos is impossible. We should not forget that in the background of each trait there are complicated

The process of natural selection cannot explain the reproductive peculiarities of marsupial animals.

The composition of the mother wallaroo's milk constantly changes according to the needs of the developing wallaroo baby. When another baby is born, it will feed on milk of a completely different composition from another dug. Such precision is truly thought provoking.

130

This aquarium in a shop window represents the idea that, in the system of rules of the animal kingdom, there is not much room for change, whereas in human culture, ideologies and social régimes may change.

genetic codes that provide mutual support. The accidental appearance of these is impossible to consider.

The kangaroo is a role model from which we can learn that the variegated and fascinating parental behaviors and ontogenetic processes in the living world are inventions of a primeval guru, who is more intelligent than we are.

Let us mention another point of interest, which also supports the above assumption. There are about a dozen families of marsupial animals known today. Altogether, there are almost two hundred such species living on earth. Among them there are a few surprising forms, the pouch of which looks downward instead of upward. The female of the South American water opossum (*Chironectes minimus*) carries her dozen or so young in a waterproof pouch. When she dives into the water, she closes her pouch opening with strong sphincters. Along the edges, long hairs and suet-like discharges contribute to the creation of a watertight pocket; thus the air gets stuck

inside the pouch and the little ones can breathe.

The pouch of the burrowing marsupial mole (*Notoryctes typhlops*), also opens downward. If it were not so and the pouch faced forward, it would be filled with earth every time the mother dug a tunnel, and the little ones would certainly have to spit out dirt all day—if they didn't smother first.

A pocket looking downward is a strange fashion, but for the water opossum and the marsupial mole it is of vital importance. How could this have evolved gradually? The pouch of an ancient species would have turned one degree to the right every 10,000 years, and slowly the "side-pocketed" mole would have evolved. And after a long, long time the "upside-down-pocketed marsupial" would have emerged. What would have protected the young ones from stifling in the meantime? Or maybe it just so happened that a fortunate accident stitched the pocket of the "unconventional marsupials" on the top and at the same time split it at the bottom. Who could believe such an assumption?

Marsupials put the opponents of the design theory in their pocket merely by their way of reproduction.

A new generation of scientists

In this chapter, we reviewed the parenting techniques of a few animals. These techniques again suggest that species have not evolved from one another. We could have also examined the upbringing, feeding, teaching, and caring of the young ones discussed in this book. But let us be satisfied with the dozens of examples we have given: they already indisputably prove that the general theory of

evolution is not verified and cannot be applied (even theoretically) in many concrete cases. Therefore, it is a theory with a flawed foundation.

As in the animal world, so too among humans, newer and newer generations succeed each other. In the animal world (as we have seen) there is not much room for change, but in human culture ideas and ideologies follow each other throughout the centuries. For thousands of years, ancient civilizations believed that the world originated from a transcendental source. Only in the last 150 years or so have some people begun to seriously consider the assumption that life and its variegated species were derived exclusively from matter. As human society became more materialistic, this unproven, yet attractive hypothesis spread throughout the world and gained its current pervasive influence on modern thought.

However, people who think more thoroughly and without prejudice can see that the basic principles of the theory of evolution are unverified and untenable. One finding after another is popping up in the diverse fields of science that contradicts the theory of evolution. It is easily conceivable that humanity will shortly return to the traditional concept about the origin of the world and living beings, even if expressed in modern form. Representatives of different disciplines of science, whose business is to seek the truth, as well as educators who consider it their primary goal to share reliable authentic knowledge, can play a major part in this shift.

Because of existential and ideological reasons, some people will probably continue to maintain their usual ideas and will loathe recognizing the change of times. But just as revolutions occur in society from time to time, they also manifest in science. Naturally, scientific revolutions do not happen overnight. It may take several decades for such transitions to occur, thus ensuring the decline of certain paradigms of thinking and the strengthening of others.

In the coming decades we can expect animated debates between "retrograde" (those who tenaciously cling to the concept of evolution) and "progressive" (those supporting

131

The ontogeny of dragonflies is in itself a small miracle. (In the picture, a southern migrant hawker hatches from the larva.)

the theory of design) scientists. If evolution is really only fabrication, with time the truth will come to light. It seems that in the field of theory, the theory of evolution has already failed, but it will take some time until the scientific society and the public discover and admit this.

We can witness that all around the world there is a new generation of scientists that rejects the dogmas of predecessors and is thinking creatively on its own. This generation may perform an overall "change of regime" in the world's thinking in connection with the origin of nature and, with the help of scientific methods, bring us back to eternal truths.

In the concluding chapter, we will touch upon a few scientific and philosophical questions. in connection with the origin and functioning of the higher intelligence mentioned in the previous chapters.

Within the larva, the "wrapped up" club-tailed dragonfly develops. The newly hatched insect functions as a perfect flying apparatus. That's impressive design and packaging!

The source
of intelligence

The Source of Intelligence

In our previous chapters we reviewed the main areas of animal behavior through analysis of interesting examples. We reviewed artful preying and protecting techniques, pleasant and unpleasant relationships between species, and different types of communication. Furthermore, we examined the mysteries of migration, the race-preserving activities of certain animals, and we also looked into a few interesting cases of developing offspring.

124

For the European robin, the red spot is a key stimulus. It attacks a bird with a red tuft of feathers sooner than it would a bird without a red spot.

Inheritance and acquisition

The focus of our attention has been the realm of instincts. We see that inherited elements, which can even be exclusive, dominate the instinctive behaviors of animals. In these "closed programs," the characteristic behavior of particular species appears even without external information or experience, and all the elements of the activity take place in a defined sequence. In certain cases, a given stimulus always triggers the same behavior. For example, the European robin (*Erithacus rubecula*), when protecting its nesting area, attacks all birds having a red crop or appearing of similar size; this behavior is automatically triggered by the sight of any red spot. Researchers call such triggers key stimuli. When these are present, a hereditary mechanism elicits the response appropriate to the key stimulus (the attack in the case of the European robin).

Other combinations of behaviors are also congenital, but their complete manifestation requires a short period of learning. Such is the development of the song of chaffinches. The ability to recognize and learn the tune, as well as the simple schema of the song, is born with the bird, but individual and population-specific song variations develop by hearing, i.e., by learning. The killing behavior of small carnivores (the elements of which become fixed in the right sequence through experience) serves as an example of how open genetic programs function. For example, the polecat (*Mustela putorius*) knows all the elements of the sequence of movements necessary to kill its prey, but it

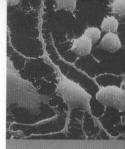

needs a short period of trying and practicing in order to learn how to put them in the right order. (For polecats encountering a rat for the first time, it takes ten to fifteen minutes to learn by experience that they can make their prey defenseless by grabbing it at its nape.) Ethologists call the ability to apply elements of behavior in a defined sequence *inherited learning mechanism*. The inexperienced polecat is "taught" the exact method of how to kill the prey by the rat itself. In these cases the animal inherits certain movements and an ability to learn which movements produce an adequate response to a given series of stimuli from the outside world. Its behavioral program is not entirely mechanistic; there are "empty" parts in it, and learning experiences "get keyed in" to domains having no information in them.

When we examined either completely ready behavioral programs or instincts completed by learning, we concluded that if one applies the principle of a step-by-step gradual evolution, it is impossible even to conceive of the emergence of the behavior characteristic of a given species. Behavioral systems are extremely complex in terms of their development and genetic background and are useful for the animal only at their full level of complexity. Therefore, so-called "previous steps" would not have provided any benefit for the animal, and thus would not have lasted. Moreover, the elements of these behavioral forms are so interdependent and complex that it is impossible that they could have emerged all at once, by accident.

Behavioral scientists try to establish an "evolutionary series" of existing species based on the complexity of their behavior. In some cases, they manage to make the superficial observer believe that they discovered the "steps of evolution." But this is just a false interpretation misleading many people, since the fact that animal behaviors may differ by degrees of complexity does not necessarily imply that the animals themselves evolved from each other. And in many cases (as our selected examples have demonstrated) it is simply impossible that forms of behavior could have transformed in such a gradual step-by-step manner. If there are behaviors that surely could not appear by evolution, it is presumable that none of them developed this way; in other words, the living world did not appear this way on earth.

The invisible center of behavior

According to prevailing notions of present-day science, genetic composition determines the behavior of living beings (just as it determines their outward appearance). The general assumption is that the combined effects of several genes cause hereditary behaviors. Cross-breeding experiments, which obviously modify the genome, showed that apart from its physical features, the animal's behavior, or the sequence of the elements in the hereditary kinetic scheme, could also change.

However, genetic research into the behavior of animals could by no means succeed in linking each of its elements to

The existence of nerve cells in itself is not an explanation for consciousness. Consciousness is a characteristic of the soul.

135

The information carriers of genes, the DNA molecules, may contain a detailed description of the living being's physical structure. The question is whether these tiny code systems could have evolved through blind biological processes.

136

definite genes. According to the prevailing hypothesis, the nervous system of animals determines each hereditary part of their behavior, while the hereditary material (DNA) codes the structure of the nervous system (the network of neurons). At present, there is no such "genome map" that would clearly show which part of the DNA sequence codes the structure of the nervous system of a particular species and how. Therefore, it is not the least certain that the hereditary knowledge that directs the animal's instinctive recognition—food acquisition, race-preservation, communication, and recognition of dangerous predators—would be contained merely in compounds. In many cases it seems simply unbelievable that the variation of the four basic compounds constituting the DNA chain (adenine, guanine, cytosine, and thymine) could record the fine details of key stimuli and inner programs directing the behavior of animals.

Is there any other way to determine behavior? Can there be information sources other than the DNA chain that direct behavior? Naturally there can be, but for this assumption, we have to detach ourselves from the stick-in-the-mud mentality of "only what we see exists."

A theory supposing a series of accidental changes in the genes by no means provides a satisfactory explanation for the origin of the different modes of behavior in the living world. Neither does it provide an explanation for the biological forms with which these behaviors are associated. *Nature's I.Q.* has pointed out that in modern biology there are many uncertainties and assertions based on bias;

thus it is possible that by their revision the modern view will in time approach the standpoint of older worldviews. Prominent representatives of modern science have already made some endeavors to come to such a synthesis of science and religion. For example, in his bestseller *Darwin's Black Box,* American professor of biochemistry Michael Behe argues that one can explain the complex molecular systems within cells only by accepting the existence of an intelligent designer. Their gradual evolution is inconceivable because organelles and intracellular mechanisms working in harmony and presupposing each other can maintain the cell only as a conjointly functioning unit; if we took anything away from it, the system would collapse.

Our approach is, that the specific appearance and behavior of different species did not evolve through millions of years from simpler beings to more complex ones. Instead, an intelligence much more refined than ours conceived and shaped the functioning of the living world in advance—from the smallest details of molecular biology to complex food chains. Not only that, the inanimate world and the whole cosmic order is also part of this intelligent design. The existing world is therefore the realization of this original, organic blueprint. This hypothesis, besides giving satisfactory answers to many basic questions, naturally raises a number of other questions, all of which we cannot answer within the limits of this book. In any case, we will address those problems and questions that we formulated at the end of previous chapters. But first let us

It seems as if the structure and functioning of the living beings of our world were determined by a preliminary, organic "design." Does it only "seem so," or it is really so?

Can we, tiny beings, learn anything about the intelligence that is beyond our world?

see what sources we can rely on in trying to answer these questions.

If a transcendental intelligence played the major role in shaping the world around us, we can actually know very little about this intelligence by our own experiences and observations. We could only ascertain that anything we see in the world has in some way or other the "impression" of this original intelligence in it. But all this tells us very little about the intelligence itself that left the trace, just as an impression of a seal tells us very little about the seal's shape and material.

Although modern science does not specifically deny the possible existence of such an immaterial and transcendental entity, most scientists do not consider inquiring about this by scientific methods to be their task. Many of these scientists accept the doctrine of methodological naturalism. For them science is limited to explaining features of the natural world

according to natural causes, without reference to any immaterial or transcendental entity. Some of these scientists may personally believe in God, but at the same time, many of them believe that God lets the world run according to natural causes alone, without any interference. Even scientists who believe that there is an intelligent designer (who manifests things not possible by natural causes alone) do not believe that the methods of modern science can reveal much about the designer. The knowledge we can gain by using scientific methods (observation, instrumental research, experiments, and logical induction) is extremely limited. For example, although governments have spent billions of dollars on space exploration, we have learned relatively very little about even the planets closest to us. Beyond these planets vast universes exist. If we cannot understand the material cosmos by scientific methods, can we believe that we can approach the realm beyond matter by these methods?

We can naturally take a skeptical standpoint and, judging such inquiry hopeless and useless, simply renounce it. But the history of thinking shows that because of our humanity, the ultimate questions of life give us no respite. Is there anything beyond the realm of matter? Does human consciousness survive in any form after the death of the body? Is there a goal to the existence of the world and man? Human nature impels us to find answers to these questions.

If we do not profess the views of some of the traditional religions in connection with these questions, we tend to invent our own answers. Even the materialistic viewpoint—according to which everything comes from matter and nothing exists apart from it—is an arbitrary answer to these questions. This notion is also not exempt from ideological prejudice. In other words, it seems that regardless of the worldview of society, because of our inquisitive nature it is impossible to avoid seeking answers to these basic philosophical questions.

His Divine Grace A. C. Bhaktivedanta Swami Prabhupada introduced the Western world to the depths of Vedic knowledge.

Answers from the past

In previous millennia, in great cultures of humanity, the worldview of the majority of society was in line with a philosophical system delineated by a particular scripture. In the Judeo-Christian culture this source has been the Bible; in Islamic countries it has been the Koran; and in the Indian subcontinent it has been the Vedic scriptures such as the *Puranas*, *Upanishads*, and other Sanskrit scriptures, which were written down, according to the tradition, some five thousand years ago.

These scriptures, disseminated by their followers, are from a transcendental source. Naturally, one can either agree or disagree with this. But whether one accepts these scriptures as infallible or

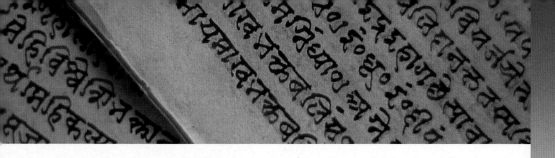

not, it is certainly exciting to explore their standpoint concerning questions that transcend the limits of our cognitive abilities.

For example, it is interesting that in connection with our subject matter, all the scriptures listed are of the opinion that the world has a personal and intelligent origin. In other words theism, or belief in God, is their main aspect. Although we may find differences in many details of their theologies, they are uniform in this respect. We cannot treat all these scriptures in depth here for obvious reasons. We will present the Indian, or Vedic, view on the origin of the world, the living beings within it, and the purpose of its existence. In doing so, we mostly rely on books written by an Indian spiritual teacher, His Divine Grace A. C. Bhaktivedanta Swami Prabhupada, who made this sublime philosophy widely available for western readers in his oeuvre of nearly sixty volumes from the late 1960s onward. We have been studying this rich corpus of Vedic knowledge for over a decade, comparing it to the scientific knowledge and scientific hypotheses of our age.

We have chosen the thesaurus of the wisdom of Indian culture as the supporting document for our assertions about a divine intelligence for several reasons. First, because of its geographic and cultural distance, scriptures of Vedic wisdom are perhaps less known to the Western audience; thus from the point of view of knowledge acquisition, their presentation is therefore useful. We have also chosen this literature because these

Sanskrit texts present in detail a supportable and logical alternative to the prevailing evolutionist view.

The structure of living beings

Let us first see what the Vedic literature tells us about living beings. What is remarkable about these texts is that they mention not only different biological forms but also the constitutional self of living beings—the soul—as well as the mind, which functions as an intermediary between the soul and the body.

According to the Vedic outlook, life itself is a symptom of the soul. While a soul is present in a particular material body, that body seems to be living, but in reality, matter is always dead, regardless of how complex it is. The living body is able to receive and respond to stimuli only because of the soul's presence; devoid of the soul, it is just a dead body, showing no phenomena of life. (Near-death experiences, during which people often experience awareness independent of their physical body, provide evidence consistent with the idea that consciousness is separate from the body.) Thus, according to the Vedic view, the soul is our true identity, our true self. And this is true not only for humans. In every animal and plant the same kind of soul exists as in human bodies.

Besides the body and the soul, Indian scriptures also mention the mind, which they describe as a subtle, invisible aspect of matter. Scientific work, such as the experiments of Robert Jahn, former dean of the Princeton University School of Engineering, has hinted at the existence of this mind

Just as the sun spreads its light all over the sky, the soul illumines the body with beams of consciousness.

140

element. Jahn's experiments showed that people by mental intention alone are able to influence the output of random number generators. The mind is the seat of the living entity's thoughts, feelings, and manifestations of will. The mind—and this is of no minor interest from the point of view of our book—is also the center of instinctive behaviors. In other words, according to the Vedic view, our thoughts are not a result of the mysterious linkages of the brain cells but products of a higher, subtle level of existence. The brain is only a secondary intermediary that forwards commands to the body coming from the soul and the mind.

Living beings populating our world thus consist of the trinity of the physical body made up of cells, the subtler mind, and the immaterial, transcendental soul.

Journey through the bodies

Teachings on the transmigration of the soul are an integral part of Indian thinking. But apart from generalities, details of this complex philosophy are not well known.

As we have explained, the eternal, indestructible soul and the temporary body are distinct entities. The bodies of living beings undergo countless changes even during one lifetime: they are born, grow, become stable, produce offspring, dwindle, and finally die. The embodied soul thus constantly "migrates" within its body, from childhood to youth to old age. According to Vedic scripture, just as the soul remains the same person

Tiny souls originate from a supreme spiritual person, just as sparks originate from fire. These spiritual sparks give life to varieties of material bodies.

while going through these changes in a lifetime, it remains the same person when it moves into another body after death. To use a simile of the *Bhagavad-gita*: living beings, or souls, change their worn-out bodies as one takes off worn-out clothes and puts on new ones. There is a body of scholarly evidence favoring this view. It comes from psychiatric reports of past life memories, such as those documented by the late University of Virginia psychiatrist Dr. Ian Stevenson and his coworkers.

Near-death experiences recorded all over the world provide evidence that consciousness functions independently from the body. When such phenomena occur, patients see their body from an external point.

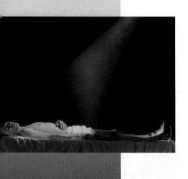

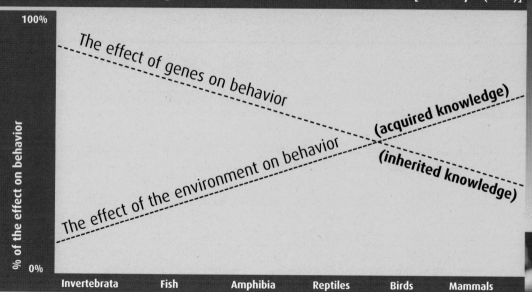

The relation of the effects of genetic and environmental factors on behavior [After Mayer (1981)]

100%

The effect of genes on behavior

(acquired knowledge)

(inherited knowledge)

The effect of the environment on behavior

% of the effect on behavior

0%

| Invertebrata | Fish | Amphibia | Reptiles | Birds | Mammals |

According to Vedic philosophy, not only humans but animals and plants also take part in the cycle of the transmigration of souls. Souls in their original spiritual environment are in full knowledge, but on coming to the material world and accepting material bodies, they forget their identity as souls; this polluted consciousness is just like a raindrop becoming muddy after falling to the ground. In the course of their migration, they experience one existence after another in different bodies. First they receive bodies with adequate intelligence to understand their spiritual identity. If they do not take advantage of such opportunities, they enter into the bodies of the world's most simple unicellular forms. After having spent their lives as protozoa, they gradually transmigrate upward through countless vegetable and animal species to human existence.

In the Vedic view, evolution in the way people understand it today never took place. The soul, however, does ascend to higher levels while assuming bodies of increasingly complex living beings. However, this is not a development of forms but of the conscious self, a development we may call "spiritual evolution." Souls dwelling in simpler bodies are reborn in higher and higher species until they are born as humans.

According to ethologists, complex living beings differ from simple ones in that their behavior is influenced more by environmental factors than by genetic determination. Let us consider the above diagram. The horizontal axis shows the categories of insects, fish, reptiles, birds, and mammals, one after the other. The vertical axis

The soul gradually transmigrates to higher and higher forms of life. It first takes on bodies of aquatic animals, then those of plants. Then it is born again and again as different kinds of insects, amphibians, reptiles, birds and mammals. Finally it gets a human body, in which it is able to shape its future fate.

The consciousness of souls inhabiting different kinds of bodies manifest in different ways. Some species have more outstanding intellectual abilities in certain fields than others.

shows the extent to which genes (hereditary behaviors) and environmental effects (the ability of adaptation and learning) have an influence on the given group of animals. The obviously simplistic diagram shows that the determining role of genes gradually decreases from insects to humans, while the ability of learning, or intelligence, gradually increases. Very simple beings, like protozoa, behave almost like machines, while bodies at a higher level allow a clearer and more advanced state of consciousness for the soul. We can characterize each species by its specific mental limits and ability to learn (although these may vary to some extent within a species). We can see the characteristics of different species, for example, by how easily some animal species learn certain activities while others cannot learn them.

The *Bhagavad-gita* also describes the differing degrees of development of the intelligence of living beings, although in different wording. By the help of expressive analogies, it shows the degrees to which matter covers the originally pure consciousness of the soul. Certain living beings, says the *Bhagavad-gita,* are enveloped by illusion as a fetus is enveloped by the womb. This "tight packing" refers to the almost unconscious existence of plants. A thinner layer of matter covers the consciousness of animals, another group of living beings, as dust covers a mirror. The consciousness of human beings is compared to fire covered by smoke. Although smoke is translucent, such a consciousness also results in a covered existence, compared to the original condition of the pure soul.

In summary, what happens in the process of reincarnation is that the soul, which fell to lower levels of existence, is gradually elevated from a state of complete envelopment by illusion to more advanced levels of consciousness. Its intelligence opens more and more, and it progresses from darkness to the light of human intelligence.

Evolution—from top to bottom

As we have seen, according to the Vedic view, the different types of animal bodies exist without changing. However, it would only be proper to ask how these forms appeared, if not by the self-organization of matter, i.e., evolution. Vedic philosophy has an exhaustive answer to this question, too, briefly presented here.

The process of how biological bodies appeared in our world could be best termed inverse evolution or devolution. The expression indicates that the direction of the process is exactly the opposite of what the well-known Darwinian explanation supposes. That is, Darwin thought that more complex living beings evolved from simpler ones by changes occuring over many thousands of years. According to the theory of Vedic devolution, all this takes place in exactly the reverse order: forms of our world come into being with the help of living beings more complex than we are.

The Vedic idea is fundamentally theistic, i.e., it accepts a personal God as the origin of the world and living beings. The first

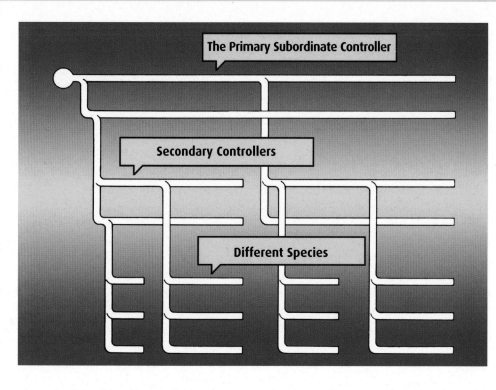

element of the "devolutionary" genealogical line is precisely this Supreme Being. Naturally the question immediately arises, "Where does he come from?" Indian scriptures tell us that this original being—quite inconceivable for the limited human mind—has always existed, from time immemorial, independent of anything else. (In all religions, a common conception of God is that he *is* the source of everything.) If we think about it, this is no less credible than the scientific assumption that the world came into being by a huge explosion from an infinitely compact point, the origin of which we know nothing about. The assumption of a conscious origin of the world is even more consistent in that it gives a reasonable explanation for the incredible order and harmony in our world.

The Vedic account of the origin of species has three main principles: existence of a supreme person, living beings on other planets with special creative and multiplication abilities, and descent by modification.

The mind of the Supreme Being is the source of the plan for the creation of all the cosmos and every species of life. However, he does not create them directly. From this supreme entity springs the first living being, called Brahma. He inherits the plan of the subsequent species and becomes the "created creator." He also employs mediators. According to the Vedic view, life exists on other planets. Brahma lives in the highest planetary system of the universe. Special superhuman creatures are born from him

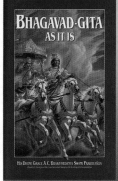

with unusual abilities. They have the knowledge and capacity to reach other places of the cosmos and beget different types of living beings there.

In this sense, the Vedic account of the origin of living beings shares some of the features of the Darwinian evolutionary theory—descent from a common ancestor and a process of reproduction with modification. This differs from the theory of special creation, held by some religionists, which involves the Supreme Being creating each species separately.

The idea of "life on other planets" is not completely strange to modern science. For example, Francis Crick (who along with James Watson discovered the double-helix structure of DNA) found the genetic code so complex that he proposed the extraterrestrial origin of the living beings on earth ("directed panspermia" theory).

In a given period, not all possible species are present on earth, and because of the alternation of settlement and devastation, the composition of the fauna and flora also changes periodically. This explains why paleontological and archeological research shows that over long periods of the history of the earth the composition of the vegetable and animal kingdom changes.

Some pending questions

As indicated at the end of previous chapters, in analyzing the subject matter of this book, we left a few questions unanswered in connection with the methodology of intelligent design:

- What made a supreme, intelligent being conceive and create animals with the shapes and behaviors known to us?
- For what purpose do all beings feed on other living beings and have well-confinable food-capturing abilities?
- Why did this superior being design the animals with varied abilities to defend themselves, and at the same time, why did he render them defenseless against nature?
- Why did he "unite" different species by making them participants of variegated symbiotic and parasitic relationships?
- What could be the purpose of the supposed designer in creating communication systems for animals to assist with self-preservation and race preservation?
- Why is it that certain species have special abilities (instinct) for orientation and migration?
- What is the need for the different strategies of reproduction and parental care of animals?
- Why do plants and animals exist, and why does the human race exist?

The Vedic scriptures state that each soul comes from a perfect and eternally existing spiritual world, which it left out of curiosity. The soul is curious to know and enjoy the world made of matter. The material bodies it subsequently takes make it possible for the soul to experience the joys and sorrows of this world in as many ways as possible and, upon reaching the human form of life, to have the opportunity to liberate itself from the control of matter.

The soul fallen into the material world becomes part of the process of transmigration described above. Since it came into this world because it wants to control and enjoy it, the various bodies that it accepts one after another provide the soul with various opportunities to exercise a certain type of power and to experience mundane enjoyment. The multitude of experiences the soul undergoes in the various species serves the completeness of its experiment with matter.

The biological forms, instincts, and mental capacities of living beings are the arrangement of a supreme, intelligent being. He shaped each species in accordance with the circumstances ordained for them. He set their type of food and the methods of its acquisition, as well as their ways of protecting themselves from aggressors. He put the species together in a certain order, in which there are several types of relationships: neutral coexistence, parasitism, mutually beneficial symbiosis, etc. So that they may effectively fulfill their roles during their lives, he set special communication systems for each species. He designed various migration routes and yearly schedules for them, aimed at helping them survive and reproduce. He also equipped them with the instinct of race preservation, the knowledge necessary for it, and the ability to take care of their offspring. The reason for the necessity of a continuous replacement of the generations of species is to provide appropriate types of "bodily vehicles" for souls of differing levels of consciousness.

When souls transmigrate into the bodies of living beings of ever-more complex structure, the minds that go together with them provide for the possibility of an even higher level of consciousness. The living being attains the highest level of consciousness when, after millions of years of evolution through lower species, reaches the human form of life. In lower forms of life it was driven mostly by its instincts and was able to use its abilities only as encoded, but the

145

While contemplating the wonders of nature one cannot help but ask the question: What is the purpose of the existence of living beings, and what is the purpose of our own existence?

The praying mantis has prayed well: a careless insect has just flown near it. In the material world, there is a constant fight: the weaker become victims of the stronger.

human body allows an almost complete development of the soul's original consciousness. Humans have consciousness, can think philosophically, and thanks to their open communication system (speech), can express their feelings and ideas unlimitedly. Within this world, certainly humans have the greatest freedom. But this entails that they are also responsible for their acts. Vedic texts explain this responsibility, known as the law of karma, in detail. The essence is that every action of a human being brings forth a reaction that is contrary in direction but similar in quantity to the act committed. In other words, if we perform an act that is beneficial to another, someone will

help us in a similar way in this life or a future life. And if we harm someone, including members of subhuman species, we will undergo a similar suffering in the future. Since we act almost continually during our life, good and bad reactions accumulate and, from time to time, fructify in the form of favorable and unfavorable events in our lives.

The moral level of human beings influences their next birth. Because animals cannot exercise free will, they automatically elevate to more developed species in the process of transmigration. However, the souls living in human bodies receive their next body according to their deeds. They can elevate themselves to the spiritual world or species in realms superior to our earthly existence, or they can receive a human body again with more or less facility for enjoyment or suffering. (For example, a poor person may take birth in a wealthy family.) But they can also fall back to the level of animal or vegetal existence if that is what they deserve through their actions. The important thing is the consciousness they developed during their human existence. The state of consciousness at death determines what body they will get in their next incarnation. If the main goal of their life was to attain their real spiritual identity, and they lived a regulated, moral, and religious life accordingly, they can return to their original eternal existence in the spiritual world. If they acted mostly piously but remained attached to material enjoyment, they can take birth again as humans. And if they merely strengthened their animalistic desires and wasted the valuable opportunity of human birth, their chance to

elevate their consciousness by making steps conducive to spiritual advancement, then according to their desires and deeds they descends into lower forms of life.

A farewell to the reader

We have no other task left than to summarize the contents of this book and bid farewell to the reader.

Contrary to the popular idea that the living forms in this world evolved spontaneously, without any higher control, abundant phenomena around us—like the behavior of animals—strongly indicate that our world was designed and created by a supernatural, intelligent being of amazing knowledge and abilities. In reality, nature's I.Q. is the creator's I.Q. We are convinced that this realization could change not only scientific thinking, but could also enhance the development of a new view of nature in the whole of humanity.

The basis of this view is that everything in nature is the result of and evidence for the working of a transcendental intelligence. According to this view, we are not the proprietors and the ultimate controllers, but only "caretakers" of this world, whose responsibility is to ensure that human society works in harmony with the desire of this higher intelligence. Another result of this view, for example, is love for all living beings and understanding the equality of souls. We hope this can help humanity to live in harmony with the divine laws of nature and create a peaceful world where everyone has the opportunity to fulfill the goal of human life and thus reach the happiest state of existence. If the majority of people were conscious of this goal, we would not think the main purpose of civilization is to create more technologically advanced tools, while damaging more and more of our natural environment for our bodily comfort and gratifying our senses.

The events of animal life manifest as eating, sleeping, defending, and mating. If we, as human beings, preoccupy ourselves with only these activities, then ultimately

The soul, after a long wandering in the material world, returns to its original home, the company of God.

148

Nature is seen in a different light and life lived differently, when we realize that behind this entire world there is a higher intelligence.

we are hardly better than animals. We all feel and know that humans have a greater purpose than lower living beings. The Vedic scriptures encourage us to search for this purpose and to use our valuable intelligence to seek the truth.

In our chapters on the animal kingdom, we noted the groundless basis for the hypothesis that all phenomena in the living world came into being by evolution. In light of this, we ask that readers at least acknowledge that the Darwinian theory of evolution is not a proven fact but merely a hypothesis that includes numerous logical difficulties. We respect the right to believe in Darwinism, but do not think it rightful that educational institutions and those who popularize scientific knowledge present evolution as a proven fact. In our opinion, this is an ideological manipulation that violates the principle of ideological neutrality of science. For unbiased information,

biology students should have the opportunity to learn about the critiques and alternatives of evolution as well.

In the last chapter of our book, we outlined one such ancient alternative to show that there is a real choice concerning the origin of the living world. Everyone can choose between evolutionism, the intelligent design theory that is currently gaining ground in the scientific community, or the explanation of the world's origin found in any of the scriptures of the world's religions. We can make a decision only with full knowledge of the alternatives, and can thus avoid being forced into the frames of a particular system of thinking. It is for this purpose that we have presented the fundamental principles of Vedic philosophy. We hope our book appeals to the soul at least as much as it appeals to the intelligence. Thank you for accompanying us on this investigation.

Bibliography,
List of Pictures, Index

Bibliography

Attenborough, David, *A madarak élete (The Life of Birds)*, Kossuth Kiadó, Budapest, 1999.

Attenborough, David, *Élet a Földön (Life on Earth)*, Park Könyvkiadó, Budapest, 1994.

Attenborough, David, *Az élet erőpróbái (The Trials of Life)*, Park Könyvkiadó, Budapest, 1991.

Bailey, Jill, *Halak (Fish)*, Helikon Kiadó, Budapest, 1992.

Bálint, Andor, *Az öröklés- és származástan alapjai (The Foundations of Genetics and Phylogenetics)*, Mezőgazdasági Kiadó, Budapest, 1977.

Behe, Michael J., Darwin's Black Box, Free Press, Budapest, 1996.

Bradley, Walter L., Roger Olsen and Charles B. Thaxton, *The Mystery of Life's Origin*, Philosophical Library Publishers, New York, 1984.

Brewster, Bernice et al., Guiness, *Különleges állatok (Guiness Book of Animal Records)*, Solaris Kft., Budapest, 1990.

Bright, Michael et al., *A természet megfejtett titkai (Looking into Nature's Secrets)*, Reader's Digest Kiadó Kft., Budapest, 1997.

Buzsáki, György, *Az állatok tanulása (The Way Animals Learn)*, Natura, Budapest, 1984.

Carwardine, Mark, *Bálnák és delfinek (Whales and Dolphins)*, Panem Kft., Budapest, 1995.

Carwardine, Mark, Guinness, *Állatrekordok (The Guinness Book of Animal Records)*, Aquila Könyvkiadó, Budapest, 1999.

Cremo, Michael A.and Richard L. Thompson, *Az emberi faj rejtélyes eredete (The Hidden History of the Human Race)*, Govinda Kft., Budapest, 2000.

Csányi, Vilmos, *Az állatok tanulása a természetben (The Learning of Animals in Nature)*, Natura Könyvkiadó, Budapest, 1987.

Csányi,Vilmos, *Etológia (Ethology)*, Nemzeti Tankönyvkiadó, Budapest, 1994.

Darwin, Charles, *A fajok eredete (The Origin of Species)*, Typotex, Budapest, 2000.

Denton, Michael, *Evolution: A Theory in Crisis*, Adler and Adler Publishers Inc., Bethesda, Md., 1986.

Downer, John, *SuperNatural*, BBC Worldwide, London 1999.

Dröscher, Vitus B., *Vándorutak az állatvilágban [Migration Paths in the Animal World]*, Tessloff és Babilon Kiadó, Budapest, 1991.

Dröscher, Vitus B.: *Ahogy az állatok látnak, hallanak és éreznek [The Way Animals See, Hear and Feel]*, Tessloff és Babilon Kiadó, Budapest, 1990.

Elphick, Jonathan (ed.), *A madárvonulás atlasza (Atlas of Bird Migration)*, Cser Kiadó, Budapest, 1996.

Farkas, Henrik, *Változó állatvilág [The Changing World of Animals]*, Gondolat, Budapest, 1978.

Farkas, Henrik, *Vándorló állatvilág [Migrating Animals]*, Gondolat, Budapest, 1980.

Ferell, Vance, *The Wonders of Nature*, Harvestime Books, Altamont, USA, 1996.

Gitt, Werner and K. H. Vanheiden, *Ha az állatok beszélni tudnának (If Animals Could Talk)*, Evangéliumi Kiadó és Iratmisszió, Budapest, 1991.

Greguss, Ferenc, *Eleven találmányok [Living Inventions]*, Móra Ferenc Könyvkiadó, Budapest, 1982.

Harrison, Colin and Alan Greensmith, *A világ madarai (Birds of the World)*, Panem Kft., Budapest, 1995.

Karádi, Ilona and Kőnig Frigyes, *Különös állatok [Extraordinary Animals]*, Móra Ferenc Könyvkiadó, Budapest, 1985.

Koroknay, István, *Érdekes állatvilág [The Interesting World of Animals]*, Aranyhal Könyvkiadó, Budapest, w.o.d.

Lange, Erich, *Metamorfózisok az állatvilágban [Metamorphoses in the Animal World]*, Gondolat, Budapest, 1988.

Lányi, György, *A természet szabadalmai [Nature's Patents]*, Gondolat, Budapest, 1978.

Lányi, György, *Meglepő dolgok állatokról [Surprising Things about Animals]*, Gondolat, Budapest, 1980.

Lorenz, Konrad, *Összehasonlító magatartás-kutatás. Az etológia alapjai (The Foundations of Ethology. The Principal Ideas and Discoveries in Animal Behavior)*, Gondolat, Budapest, 1985.

Majer, József, *Hogyan viselkednek az állatok? [How Do Animals Behave?]*, Tankönyvkiadó, Budapest, 1981.

Morris, Desmond, *Állatlesen (Animal Watching: A New Guide to the Animal World)*, Európa Könyvkiadó, Budapest, 1992.

Prabhupada, A. C. Bhaktivedanta Swami, *A Bhagavad-gita, úgy, ahogy van (The Bhagavad-gita As It Is)*, Bhaktivedanta Book Trust, Budapest, 1993.

Reichholf-Riehm, Helgard, *Rovarok és pókszabásúak [Insects and Spiders]*, Magyar Könyvklub, Budapest, 1996.

Remane, Adolf, *Az állatok társas viselkedése [The Social Behavior of Animals]*, Natura, Budapest, 1978.

Siku, Andrea, I*nverz evolúció [Inverse Evolution]*, Tejút Bt., Budapest, 1997.

Slater, J. B. Peter, *Az állatok társas viselkedése (Essentials of Animal Behavior)*, Helikon Kiadó, Budapest, 1992.

Slater, J. B. Peter, *Bevezetés az etológiába (Introduction to Ethology)*, Mezőgazdasági Kiadó, Budapest, 1987.

Spellerberg, Ian F. Et al., *Különleges állatok (Usborne Mysteries and Marvels of the Reptile World)*, Solaris Kft., Budapest, 1990.

Steinmann, Henrik, *Társak és ellenségek az állatvilágban [Partners and Enemies in the Animal World]*, Natura Könyvkiadó, Budapest, 1985.

Steinmann, Henrik, *Az állatok násza [Nuptials in the Animal World]*, Natura Könyvkiadó, Budapest, 1980.

Sterbetz, István, *A nagy parancs [The Big Command]*, Móra Ferenc Könyvkiadó, Budapest, 1985.

Storch, Volker and Ulrich Welsch, *Evolúció [Evolution]*, Springer Hungarica Kiadó Kft., Debrecen, 1995.

Szalkay, József, *Rovarok között [Among Insects]*, Mezőgazdasági Kiadó, Budapest, 1971.

Széky, Pál, *Etológia [Ethology]*, Natura, Budapest, 1979.

Széky, Pál, *Állat az állatnak üzen [Animal Messages]*, Natura, Budapest, 1986.

Szinák, János and Veress István, *Üvöltés az éjszakában [A Howl in the Night]*, Gondolat, Budapest, 1985.

Tasi, István, *Ahol megáll a tudomány [Where Science Stops]*, Lál Kiadó, Somogyvámos, 1999.

Tasi, István (ed.), *Darwin alkonya? [Darwin's Sunset?]* Tattva periodical, Budapest, 1999.

Terofal, Fritz, *Tengeri halak [Sea Fish]*, Magyar Könyvklub, Budapest, 1996.

Tóth, Gábor (ed.), *Darwin majmot csinált belőlünk? [Has Darwin Made a Monkey of Us?]*, Gauranga Média, Budapest, 1999.

Uránia állatvilág, Alsóbbrendű állatok; *Halak, kétéltűek, hüllők; Madarak; Emlősök [Inferior Animals; Fish, Amphibia and Reptiles; Birds; Mammals]*, Gondolat, Budapest, 1969–77.

Whitfield, Philip, *Az állatok képes enciklopédiája (The Simon and Schuster Encyclopedia of Animals: A Visual Who's Who of the World's Creatures)*, Magyar Könyvklub, Budapest, 1999.

151

152

List of Pictures

Special thanks to the following photographers for the
selfless help:

Ákos Hivekovics, Zsolt Kalotás, István Kerekes, Tibor
Molnár, Vilmos Pőcze, Géza Ruppert, György Simon,
János Vajda, András Vojnits.

The pictures not listed above are from Digital Vision
Collection: Amazing Creatures and Corel Gallery: Animals.

Index

155

159

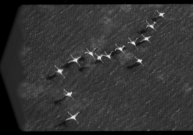